HUMAN REALIZATION
AN INTRODUCTION TO THE PHILOSOPHY OF MAN

JOHN F. KAVANAUGH, S.J.

CORPUS BOOKS

New York/Cleveland

CORPUS BOOKS

Editorial Offices:
110 East 59th Street
New York, New York 10022

Sales & Distribution
2231 West 110th Street
Cleveland, Ohio 44102

First Printing 1970

Library of Congress Catalog Card Number: 73-100977

Contents

PREFACE

CHAPTER ONE: The Philosophical Enterprise   1

   The Discipline of Questioning   3
   The Discipline of Liberation   5
   The Discipline of Personhood   7
   Reading: "What Is Philosophy?" Karl Jaspers   11
   Notes   17
   Bibliography   18

CHAPTER TWO: The Drive to Understand   22

   The Level of Immediacy: Sense Knowledge   24
   The Level of Distance: Transcending Immediacy   28
   The Unity of Knowledge and the Radical
      Openness of Man   32
   Readings: "Hymn of the Universe,"
      Pierre Teilhard de Chardin   36
      "I and Thou," Martin Buber   38
   Notes   40
   Bibliography   42

CHAPTER THREE: The Drive to Do Something
      About It   44

   The Levels of Wanting: Sensorial and Intellectual   46
   Love of the Other for His Own Sake   48
   The Unity of Human Powers in the Total Person   51
   The Soul: Radical Basis of Unity in a Person   53
   Reading: "Some Basic Propositions of a Growth
      and Self-Actualization Psychology,"
      Abraham Maslow   56
   Notes   61
   Bibliography   63

CHAPTER FOUR: Human Freedom   65

Phenomenological Analysis of Reflection and
   Questioning   67
Free Choice: A Metaphysical Analysis of the Will   70
The Position of Total Determinism   72
The Case for Absolute Freedom   77
Structured Freedom: Human Reality   81
A Note on Freedom and Anxiety   83
Reading: "Freedom of Consciousness," John Wild   87

Notes   93

Bibliography   96

CHAPTER FIVE: The Drive to Give Oneself Away   100

The Human Potentialities of Sexual Love   103
Reading: "The Metaphysics of Love,"
   F. D. Wilhelmsen   115

Notes   119

Bibliography   121

CHAPTER SIX: The Unfolding of Open Potentialities:

The Human Soul   123
The Metaphysical Argument   127
The Phenomenological Argument   129
The Meanings of Death   131
The Naturalist's Approach   133
The Approach of Some Existentialists   134
The Religious Dualism Approach   137
Man as Openness to the Fullness of Being   138
A Note on Revelation   143
Readings: "The Scandal of Truth," Jean Daniélou   145
   "Theism and Materialism," William James   146

Notes   149

Bibliography   153

Index   155

Chapter One

The Philosophical Enterprise

"I suffer thirst, Govinda, and on this long Samana path my thirst has not grown less. I have always thirsted for knowledge. I have always been full of questions. Year after year I have questioned the Brahmins, year after year I have questioned the holy Vedas . . . . I have spent a long time and have not yet finished, in order to learn this, Govinda: that one can learn nothing. There is, so I believe, in the essence of everything, something that we cannot call learning. There is, my friend, only a knowledge—that is everywhere, that is Atman, that is in me and you and in every creature, and I am beginning to believe that this knowledge has no worse enemy than the man of knowledge, than learning."[1]

Hermann Hesse

Perhaps the greatest service to philosophy would be to change its name. The very tone of the word itself calls to mind a vast spectrum of meanings, most of which seem dark, remote, and even unworthy of consideration. We might picture an isolated thinker, within the walls of his room, trying to save the appearances of a world which he does not understand. A great system-builder might come to mind, one who has now been relegated to abstruse footnotes and erudite commentaries. Or, more immediately, we might conceive lists of

1

philosophical courses imposed upon us by the academicians who seem to have little contact at all with the demands of the present.

These are only some of the notions which a person might carry with himself when he confronts the discipline of philosophy today. He may often spend his time going through the useless motions of a formal education in order to be handed an equally useless sheet of onion-skinned paper which is somehow supposed to validate his existence. A great part of his formal education will have been made up of what has been called philosophy, in which he memorized answers to questions which he himself had never asked—or perhaps, which never should have been asked by anyone in the first place. He will have taken philosophy courses which most often had turned out being mistakes on all levels—experientially, pedagogically, and humanistically.

And so it is often the case with all of us. We seem to study the philosophy of man in grand isolation from the sociological, psychological, and behavioral sciences. We see little connection between philosophy and history, myth, literature, or mystery. Philosophy must be a "science," a respectable discipline with subjects and credentials of its own. We are often expected to be more concerned with the problems of "the one and the many," the development of logical atomism, and linguistic or metaphysical analyses than with the problem of the philosopher himself who once thought it important to question his meaning and the horizon of his potentialities as a man. And just as frequently, we spend our time trying to remember what a philosopher said, rather than trying to understand what drove the philosopher to *want* to say anything in the first place.

This is not in the least to make an indictment of all that has gone before us, or to set up a straw man who will later be destroyed by our own brilliance. Rather, we want to make sure that we first know *why* we are driven to philosophy as a sheer human exigency. To begin with, why do we question at all; what is involved in the act of questioning; and what are the primordial questions that we ask? Consequently, before we even begin to talk about the community of great minds or the perennial philosophical problems, we must first come to the realization that philosophy is at root the pre-eminently personal affair of question-asking.

The Discipline of Questioning

The act of questioning, of wanting to know, is the initiation to philosophy. And most fundamental here are the immediate data that I discover about myself in this very act of initiation—I want to know who and what I am. I want to know and understand my identity. This is what we might call the beginnings of a philosophy of man, in which we try to discover the meaning of the self, of man, of the questioner. We must ask ourselves what the significance of questioning, of wanting, and of knowing actually is. Does questioning imply a liberation from and drive out of the confines of the self? Does questioning imply an immediate fundamental relatedness to what is other than the self? Does questioning demand a self—transcending ground for its impetus and intelligibility?

Following these questions, if I come to an understanding of my identity as a man and of my potentialities as a questioner, I will be almost necessarily led to the realm of behavior and action. For a man to ask of himself, "What am I to do?" he must first know who he is and what he can be; and for a man to act morally, he must act in accordance with his understanding of what his true identity and potentialities are. In following this out he might be led to ask whether questioning itself might be seen as the basic human demand for value in the world. Will the understanding of himself as a knowing, loving, related being actually become the immediate basis of value in his life and the standard of his behavior? And at this point, the reflective person is thrust into what might be called the world of ethics.

Moreover, there are many other worlds open to the questioner. He might ask what it *means* to question, why he is driven to question, what it means to be without all the answers, or what it means actually to be, rather than not be at all. He might ultimately ask why there is a *must* quality to his questioning and whether his insatiable drive to question demands an inexhaustible ground of and response to his identity as a questioner.

All of this is merely to say that philosophy begins with the questioning self—not in the sense that we are looking for an absolutely indubitable starting point, but in the sense that any starting point must be experientially authenticated. It is not in the spirit of morbid introspection or egocentricity that the philosopher begins with the self; it is rather in the spirit of the Socratic imperative to know oneself that he begins there. In fact, the philosopher's conclusion might well be that the self is truly found in exocentric dynamisms.

Likewise, our emphasis upon the self and its identity is not meant to imply that philosophical community, precision, and discipline are not necessary. If the philosophical community and its heritage are ignored, a basic denial of one's identity and historicity is operative. We could never hope, nor should we want to hope, for a vacuum from which we might begin. If this were the case, a beginning might never be made. Similarly, without careful analysis and exacting reflection, our insights and conclusions could most probably turn into sheer conjecture, sentimentality, or philosophical warm blankets. It is not just a question of feeling good about life, nor is it a question of pursuing relevance; rather the philosophical enterprise is one of pursuing truth. For it is the truth of what one actually is which will set one free—be it palatable or not, be it a comfort or a threat.

With all of these considerations and provisos made, however, it remains true that philosophy would never have come into existence had it not been the most personal of human endeavors. In this sense, if philosophy is to die, humanity will whither away not long after. Cessation of questioning can only bring stagnation and the arresting of growth. That is why philosophy as we understand it here is so radically important. Its grandeur does not lie in the fact that great systems have been and will be constructed. Its achievement is not that some perennial "melody-line" has dominated all of western man's thought. Rather, philosophy's greatness lies in the individual philosopher's drive toward the truth; it is in the complexity of "takes" upon the reality in which we are immersed and through which we live; it is the music of the fugue with the incessant counterpoint of questioning and answering. And it did not begin with an answer.

4

The Philosophical Enterprise
The Discipline of Liberation

At an even more fundamental level, philosophy as a discipline of questioning implies a release—perhaps even a revolt—from historical, sociological, and psychological encapsulation. By the very fact that a question arises, I am liberated from the chains of unquestioning acceptance of whatever is at hand. I can say "wait a second" to the present situation or the status quo. I am able to place myself at distance from the press of all the data and stimuli that are immediately beckoning me. And what is more, I can resist the currents which pull me toward thoughtless conformity.

In philosophical questioning, then, I am liberated from blind adherence to what is present or what is promised as reward. A horizon of possibilities rather than necessity is before me. To the reflective mind, the society in which he lives is no longer an imprisoning womb offering the cessation of growth with its gifts of security and status. His faith in man or God is no longer adhered to or dismissed out of tyrannizing fear or moral authoritarianism. Rather, the world around the questioning philosopher is an invitation to be listened to and responded to. By placing himself at a distance from his environment, his historicity, and his pre-philosophical prejudices, the reflective man can be said to be effecting a personal revolt at its most radical level.

Herein the philosopher initiates a revolution, not of negation, but of affirmation—by opening himself to the fullest possibilities that might be offered to him. His movement is not one of refusal to recognize the past and present structures, for these are part of his very identity as a historical event; rather philosophical revolt is a breaking out of the confines of those structures when they threaten to become a priori necessities which close viable avenues to the truth.

Therefore, since personal philosophical revolution is the affirmation of one's self possession, only a failure in fidelity to the basic openness which questioning entails could possibly lead to a stifling of the self in hopeless negation. Quite to the contrary, the purified act of philosophical revolt will rather lead to the construction of a personally validated world—view which emerges from the recognition of one's own selfhood.

Involved, then, in the concept of philosophy as liberation is the moment of confronting and embracing the past which is part of us—a taking possession of it—and the equally important affirmation of the future as creative self-project. Considered in this light, philosophy is fundamentally a subversive activity, carrying the connotations of both "underneathness" (continuity) and a turning from under (organic diversification). Here is not an obsessive reaction or blind revolution against the past as some externalized threatening force. Nor do we have an acquiescent acceptance of present structures rooted in fear of precarious questioning. Rather, in subversive philosophy, there are both lines of stabilization (openness to our own historicity and to what *is*) and of fluidity (openness to what can and should be).

Perhaps if we could manage to see philosophy in this light, much of our present disenchantment would cease. We will see that it is not a question of updating any particular system or of making philosophy more scientific and objective. What one needs is the conviction that philosophy is the discipline of man's restlessness, of his drive to question in its most fundamental sense. To philosophize is to attempt to take a posture with respect to one's self and one's condition. In our realization of this fact, we will see that diversity rather than conformity or unity will be a primary characteristic of philosophy—not that truth itself is necessarily diverse, but that philosophy as a discipline of free questioners is. For once one has realized that philosophy cannot be a spectator-endeavor, one must come to grips with the fact that historicity will continually emerge within the individual's confrontation with the real world around him. Nevertheless, although one's history, environment, and disposition constantly assert themselves in reflection, one retains a methodological and philosophical vehicle for challenging them—if he remains faithful to the meaning of questioning.

Our emphasis, then, is on the process, the questioning, rather than the certified answer, as the basis of our drive to understand and our fidelity to true philosophical endeavor. Perhaps to demand absolute certainty and philosophical conformity is to present philosophy with its greatest threat, for in finding neither we may

6

trap ourselves by these very demands in a snare of futile skepticism; and on the other hand, if we claim success in achieving absolute certitude, we may be guilty of ignoring the process, growth, and incompletion of the human condition in our very flight from its contingency and temporality—and all of this is to flee from our own identity. As Marcel says in his *Philosophy of Existence*:

> *This perpetual beginning again, which may seem scandalous to the scientist or to the technician, is an inevitable part of all genuinely philosophical work; and perhaps it reflects in its own order the fresh start of every new awakening and of every birth. Does not the very structure of duration and of life show that philosophical thought is unfaithful to reality whenever it attempts to proceed from conclusion to conclusion towards a Summa which, in the end, needs only to be expounded and memorized paragraph by paragraph?*[2]

Such an insight, however, unfortunately misses many of us completely. This is why our greatest concern must be to purify the notions of philosophy we now have. Changing its name, needless to say, will not help. What is needed is the fundamental realization of its radically personal meaning grounded in the identity of the questioner himself.

The Discipline of Personhood

If I am to be a philosopher, then it is I who must philosophize. Even if there were an absolutely perfect philosophical system worked out once and for all, it would be useless to me as a reflective being unless I myself shall have done it, thought it, made it my own. For truth, whether objective or not, must be *my* truth if it is to be operative at all in my life. This is the "one thing necessary" that Kierkegaard constantly reminds us of. One's life is one's own unique creative project; and the formation of it must be grounded in the reflective understanding, interpretation, and communication of one's basic experience. Herein lies the uniqueness and originality of every philosopher.

Moreover, since I am a member of a species-event with

7

communal needs, experiences, and drives, my philosophizing will be the basis of discourse with other men. And this discourse itself will be a part of my experiential confrontation of the world; therefore it will demand listening, responding, consideration, and comparison with my own understanding of experience. With these things in mind, it becomes clear that I am not methodologically turned in upon myself. Quite the contrary, philosophical dialogue and historical study are essential parts of the manifold of total experiential date which I am to consider.

If I am able to understand my need for such discourse, I will realize that my own reflection can never be definitively finished. I am an evolutionary event, historically placed. This means not only that I am influenced by and profit from the past—whether it be the past of Plato, Augustine, Thomas, Kant, or Dewey—but that I must never stop interpreting, judging, evaluating, and building my philosophy and my creative life-project. Herein will lie my greatest accomplishment as a philosopher and as a man. This is each individual person's task, as Buber calls it, in "the actualization of his unique, unprecedented, and never-recurring potentialities, and not the repetition of something that another, and be it even the greatest, has already achieved."[3]

Such is the goal of the philosopher who begins with a question and investigates all that the dynamism of questioning implies. But in trying to solve the riddles of identity and action, he will open himself not only to his own experience and that of other philosophers, but to anything which which might be a vehicle for answering the questions of man—the world of literature, of history, of myth, and of the positive sciences. For in each of these worlds man is similarly driven to ask the primary questions: "Who am I?" and "What am I to do?"

If we look at ourselves or listen to the testimony of other men, we can see that the human person is driven, by his very personhood, to know and to do something about himself. This occurs not only in the quixotic man who wishes to "dream the impossible dream," or achieve the Grail, but also in the man who weeps over the world because there is no more to conquer and in the countless others who somehow seek to validate their meaning and their existence. All of

8

these dreams are simply the reiterations of primary questions in an intensely practical, existential manner. Every man wants to know himself and do something about himself. Whether it is with Viktor Frankl speaking of "man's search for meaning," or Eric Erikson of "identity and the life-cycle," or Rollo May of "man's search for himself," we see the fact of man's perduring self-questioning. Sociologists speak of the "organization man," the "lonely crowd," and the alienated worker. Historians record the questioning of man in Greek myth and drama, Elizabethan tragedy, legendary heroics, cults of tragic or courtly lovers, and the revolutionary promise. Goethe speaks of the Faustian man, Dostoevsky of the moral hero, Faulkner of the noble individual, and Tennessee Williams of the confused searcher. Our great film directors are epitomized in the endless questionings of Bergman, the sterile loneliness of Antonioni, and the disillusionment of Fellini. The philosophical act of questioning actually saturates our experience. One might even be led to say that the intensity of human endeavor and creativity is based upon the intensity of the quest for one's identity and purpose.

Perhaps all of this arises from the tenuousness of our existence, òur lack of rootedness, and the awareness of our contingency. Being spread out in time and space, endlessly incompleted, and consciously present to our own insufficiency, our personhood is characterized by a "calling out." But whatever the reason be, question we must—and we demand answers.

All of us in one way or another, explicit philosopher or common man, try to realize the demands of knowing and wanting that are one with our being. The drive to understand is implicit in the blandishments of power, manipulation, and influence as well as open presence to the world. The drive to do something about it is as hiddenly insatiable in our acts of appropriation and acquisition as it is in the moments of defenseless unfolding and giving. Even if we try to escape the pressure of personhood's demands, their very presence is operative in our flight to unquestioning security or non-committal tentativeness.

Whether our answers succeed or fail will depend on the discovery of that "I" of which we constantly speak. It is only when this question of the "I" is placed and its answer is pursued diligently and reflectively that some resolution might be found.

Questioning, then, is the starting point of philosophy and the continuing force behind its development. This is methodologically true because the philosophical moment cannot begin until one has questioned the present state of affairs. Psychologically, moreover, it seems to be the foundation of man's search for his own identity and meaning. Finally, in the act of questioning, I know where to begin existentially. I am a questioner, one who *wants,* one who wants to *know*, one who wants to *act* upon knowing. To all of this we might now apply the term, *person*. And now it remains for the philosopher to reflect upon what personhood means, what knowing implies about himself, and what wanting in its fullest context might entail. Thus, in seeing the dynamisms and demands of questioning, the one who philosophizes will hopefully come to know more about himself as the source and center of these activities.

Such is the philosophical enterprise, at least in part. Realizing that his philosophy must be his own, realizing that his aim is to understand, interpret, and communicate his experience, the man who has a love of wisdom, who pursues the answers to the questions of identity and action, will not reach the point of no return when, once his more immediate dreams and desires are fulfilled, he can find nothing else worth living for.

WHAT IS PHILOSOPHY?
Karl Jaspers[4]

What philosophy is and how much it is worth are matters of controversy. One may expect it to yield extraordinary revelations or one may view it with indifference as a thinking in the void. One may look upon it with awe as the meaningful endeavour of exceptional men or despise it as the superfluous broodings of dreamers. One may take the attitude that it is the concern of all men, and hence must be basically simple and intelligible, or one may think of it as hopelessly difficult. And indeed, what goes by the name of philosophy provides examples to warrant all these conflicting judgments.

For the scientific-minded, the worst aspect of philosophy is that it produces no universally valid results; it provides nothing that we can know and thus possess. Whereas the sciences in their fields have gained compellingly certain and universally recognized insights, philosophy, despite thousands of years of endeavour, has done nothing of the sort. This is undeniable: in philosophy there is no generally accepted, definitive knowledge. Any insight which for cogent reasons is recognized by all has ipso facto become scientific knowledge and ceased to be philosophy; its relevance is limited to a special sphere of the knowable.

Nor is philosophical thought, like the sciences, characterized by progressive development. Beyond any doubt, we are far more advanced than Hippocrates, the Greek physician. But we are scarcely entitled to say that we have progressed beyond Plato. We have only advanced beyond his materials, beyond the scientific findings of which he made use. In philosophy itself we have scarcely regained his level.

It lies in the very nature of philosophy, as distinguished from the sciences, that in any of its forms it must dispense with the

11

unanimous recognition of all. The certainty to which it aspires is not of the objective, scientific sort, which is the same for every mind; it is an inner certainty in which a man's whole being participates. Whereas science always pertains to particular objects, the knowledge of which is by no means indispensable to all men, philosophy deals with the whole of being, which concerns man as man, with a truth which, wherever it is manifested, moves us more deeply than any scientific knowledge.

Systematic philosophy is indeed bound up with the sciences. It always reckons with the most advanced scientific findings of its time. But essentially philosophy springs from a different source. It emerges before any science, wherever men achieve awareness.

The existence of such a *philosophy without science* is revealed in several striking ways:

First: In philosophical matters almost everyone believes himself capable of judgment. Whereas it is recognized that in the sciences study, training, method are indispensable to understanding, in philosophy men generally assume that they are competent to form an opinion without preliminary study. Our own humanity, our own destiny, our own experience strike us as a sufficient basis for philosophical opinions.

This notion that philosophy must be accessible to all is justified. The circuitous paths travelled by specialists in philosophy have meaning only if they lead men to an awareness of being and of his place in it.

Second: Philosophical thought must always spring from free creation. Every man must accomplish it for himself.

A marvellous indication of man's innate disposition to philosophy is to be found in the questions asked by children. It is not uncommon to hear from the mouths of children words which penetrate to the very depths of philosophy. A few examples:

A child cries out in wonderment, "I keep trying to think that I am somebody else, but I'm always myself." This boy has touched on one of the universal sources of certainty, awareness of being through awareness of self. He is perplexed at the mystery of his I, this mystery that can be apprehended through nothing else. Questioningly, he stands before this ultimate reality.

Another boy hears the story of the Creation: In the beginning God made heaven and earth . . . and immediately asks, "What was before the beginning?" This child has sensed that there is no end to questioning, that there is no stopping place for the mind, that no conclusive answer is possible.

A little girl out walking in the woods with her father listens to his stories about the elves that dance in the clearings at night. . . "But there are no elves . . . " Her father shifts over to realities, describes the motion of the sun, discusses the question of whether it is the sun or the earth that revolves, and explains the reasons for supposing that the earth is round and rotates on its axis. . . "Oh, that isn't so," says the little girl and stamps her foot. "The earth stands still. I only believe what I see." "Then," says her father, "you don't believe in God, you can't see Him either." The little girl is puzzled for a moment, but then says with great assurance, "If there weren't any God, we wouldn't be here at all." This child was seized with the wonder of existence: things do not exist through themselves. And she understood that there is a difference between questions bearing on particular objects in the world and those bearing on our existence as a whole.

Another little girl is climbing the stairs on her way to visit her aunt. She begins to reflect on how everything changes, flows, passes, as though it had never been. "But there must be something that always stays the same . . . I'm climbing these stairs on my way to see my aunt—that's something I'll never forget." Wonderment and terror at the universal transience of things here seek a forlorn evasion.

Anyone who chose to collect these stories might compile a rich store of children's philosophy. It is sometimes said that the children must have heard all this from their parents or someone else, but such an objection obviously does not apply to the child's really serious questions. To argue that these children do not continue to philosophize and that consequently such utterances must be accidental is to overlook the fact that children often possess gifts which they lose as they grow up. With the years we seem to enter into a prison of conventions and opinions, concealments and unquestioned acceptance, and there we lose the candour of childhood. The child still reacts spontaneously to the spontaneity of life; the child feels and sees and inquires into things which soon disappear from his vision. He forgets what for a moment was revealed to him and is surprised when grownups later tell him what he said and what questions he asked.

Third: Spontaneous philosophy is found not only in children but also in the insane. Sometimes—rarely—the veils of universal occlusion seem to part and penetrating truths are manifested. The beginning of certain mental disorders is often distinguished by shattering metaphysical revelations, though they are usually formulated in terms that cannot achieve significance: exceptions are such cases as Hölderlin and Van Gogh. But anyone witnessing these revelations cannot help feeling that the mists in which we ordinarily live our lives have been torn asunder. And many sane people have, in awaking from sleep, experienced strangely revealing insights which vanish with full wakefulness, leaving behind them only the impression that they can never be recaptured. There is profound meaning in the saying that children and fools tell the truth. But the creative originality to which we owe great philosophical ideas is not to be sought here but among those great minds—and in all history there have been only a few of them—who preserve their candour and independence.

Fourth: Since man cannot avoid philosophy, it is always present: in the proverbs handed down by tradition, in popular philosophical phrases, in dominant convictions such as are embodied in the idiom of the "emancipated," in political opinions, but most of all, since the very beginnings of history, in myths. There is no escape from philosophy. The question is only whether a philosophy is conscious or not, whether it is good or bad, muddled or clear. Anyone who rejects philosophy is himself unconsciously practising a philosophy.

What then is this philosophy, which manifests itself so

14

universally and in such strange forms?

The Greek word for philosopher *(philosophos)* connotes a distinction from *sophos.* It signifies the lover of wisdom (knowledge) as distinguished from him who considers himself wise in the possession of knowledge. This meaning of the word still endures: the essence of philosophy is not the possession of truth but the search for truth, regardless of how many philosophers may belie it with their dogmatism, that is, with a body of didactic principles purporting to be definitive and complete. Philosophy means to be on the way. Its questions are more essential than its answers, and every answer becomes a new question.

But this on-the-wayness—man's destiny in time—contains within it the possibility of deep satisfaction, and indeed, in exalted moments, of perfection. This perfection never resides in formulable knowledge, in dogmas and articles of faith, but in a historical consummation of man's essence in which being itself is revealed. To apprehend this reality in man's actual situation is the aim of philosophical endeavour.

To be searchingly on the way, or to find peace and the fulfillment of the moment—these are no definitions of philosophy. There is nothing above or beside philosophy. It cannot be derived from something else. Every philosophy defines itself by its realization. We can determine the nature of philosophy only by actually experiencing it. Philosophy then becomes the realization of the living idea and the reflection upon this idea, action and discourse on action in one. Only by thus experiencing philosophy for ourselves can we understand previously formulated philosophical thought.

But we can define the nature of philosophy in other ways. No formula can exhaust its meaning and none can be exclusive. In antiquity philosophy was defined (by its object) as the knowledge of things divine and human, the knowledge of being as being, or it was defined (by its aim) as learning how to die, as the striving for happiness by the exercise of thought; as an endeavour to resemble the divine; and finally (in the broadest sense) as the knowledge of all knowledge, the art of all arts, as *the* science—confined to no

15

particular field.

Today perhaps we may speak of philosophy in the following terms; its aim is

to find reality in the primal source;

to apprehend reality in my thinking attitude toward myself, in my inner acts;

to open man to the Comprehensive in all its scope;

to attempt the communication of every aspect of truth from man to man, in loving contest;

patiently and unremittingly to sustain the vigilance of reason in the presence of failure and in the presence of that which seems alien to it.

Philosophy is the principle of concentration through which man becomes himself, by partaking of reality.

Although philosophy, in the form of simple, stirring ideas, can move every man and even children, its conscious elaboration is never complete, must forever be undertaken anew and must at all times be approached as a living whole—it is manifested in the works of the great philosophers and echoed in the lesser philosophers. It is a task which man will face in one form or another as long as he remains man.

1. Hermann Hesse, *Siddartha* (New York: New Directions, 1957), pp. 20-1

2. Gabriel Marcel, *The Philosophy of Existentialism* (New York: The Citadel Press, 1965. Fifth paperbound edition), p. 125.

3. Martin Buber, *Pointing the Way.* Cited in *The Worlds of Existentialism,* ed. by Maurice Friedman (New York: Random House, 1964), p. 167.

4. Karl Jaspers, *Way to Wisdom,* translated by Ralph Manheim (New Haven: Yale University Press, 1951), pp. 7-14. Reprinted by permission of Yale University Press.

There is quite obviously a broad spectrum of books recommended below. Some are specifically philosophical, some psychological, and some literary. They share in common, however, a concern for the meaning of the human situation, and to this extent serve as excellent introductions to philosophy. In addition, the novels of Dostoevsky, Golding, Kazantzakis, and others shed light on the problems discussed in this chapter.

Barrett, William. *Irrational Man.* Garden City, New York: Doubleday Anchor, 1959. This paperback is an excellent initiation to existentialism by an American philosopher. He treats existential currents in literature and art and a few existentialists in rather satisfying depth.

Copleston, F. C. *A History of Philosophy.* Garden City, New York: Doubleday Image. This is a multi-volumed paperback history of philosophy from the Greeks to Contemporary British. Excellent, especially if one is interested beyond mere acquaintance.

Frankl, Viktor. *Man's Search for Meaning.* New York: Washington Square Press, 1963. A little paperback telling the experiences of a concentration death camp in relation to the meaning of value, love, and man's identity.

———. *The Doctor and The Soul.* New York: Knopf, 1955. An extensive treatment of Frankl's psychological and therapeutic methods. Quite good, although the line between psychology and religious counseling becomes quite thin.

Fuller, Edmund. *Man in Modern Fiction.* New York: Vintage Books, 1949. Ostensibly concerned with modern American fiction, this paperback's greatest concern is with the dimensions and nobility of man.

Gibran, Kahlil. *The Prophet* and *Voice of the Master.* These two Bantam paperbacks are comprised of philosophical meditations in a theological vein concerning the questions of love, death, knowledge, evil, responsibility, etc. Easy to read, profound at times, but open to charges of sentimentalism.

Goldbrunner, Josef. *Cure of Mind and Cure of Soul.* Notre Dame, Ind.: University of Notre Dame Press, 1963. A thin paperback treating a depth psychologist's inquiry into the meaning and potentialities of the self as a person. The first eighty pages are especially good.

Hammarskjold, Dag. *Markings.* New York: Knopf, 1964. A past best-seller now in paperback which is made up of personal reflections by the former head of the U. N.

Hesse, Hermann. *Siddartha.* New York: New Directions Paperback, 1957. A remarkable novel by the author of *Demian* and *Steppenwolf* (both also excellent books), poetically dealing with the nature of questioning, the search for realization, and the nature of truth. The primacy of subjective experience is stressed.

Josephson, E. and M. *Man Alone: Alienation in Modern Society.* New York: Dell, 1962. An anthology comprised of writings from psychologists, sociologists, dramatists, novelists, and philosophers concerning man's alienation from himself and his meaning.

Kaufman, Walter. *From Shakespeare to Existentialism.* Garden City,

New York: Doubleday Anchor, 1960. A unique, broad, and sympathetic exposition of existential themes found in literature.

——— *Existentialism from Dostoevsky to Sartre.* New York: Meridian, 1960. An anthology to accompany the above. It has fairly long and sometimes difficult selections.

Lindbergh, Anne Morrow. *Gift From the Sea.* New York: Pantheon, 1955. A previous best-seller now in a paperback edition which is actually a fine introduction to the reflective life, treating the cycle of rest and activity; thought and motion.

Maslow, Abraham. *Toward a Psychology of Being.* Princeton, N.J.: Van Nostrand Insight, 1962. This is a book which should be used in conjunction with all of the chapters in this book. It is extremely valuable on the notions of value, forms of knowledge and love. Much, however, is based on a not-totally validated scientific hypothesis.

Matson, Floyd. *The Broken Image.* Garden City, New York: Doubleday Anchor, 1966. A humanistic approach to the psychological and sociological problems of man. Especially concerned with the problem of freedom.

May, Rollo. *Man's Search for Himself.* New York: Signet, 1967. Now in paperback, a treatment of the problem of loneliness and purposelessness in modern society. The solution is offered along the lines of integral selfhood and the potential of man for self-transcendence.

Novak, Michael. *Belief and Unbelief.* New York: Macmillan, 1968. An important recent book now in paperback which is primarily concerned with the existence of God, but the early chapters are quite informative on the implications of the self-as-questioner.

Rilke, Rainer Maria. *Letters to a Young Poet.* New York: Norton, 1963. Paperback. A beautifully literary presentation of the reflective mind and its concern for humanity.

Royce, Joseph. *The Encapsulated Man.* Princeton, N.J.: Van Nostrand Insight, 1964. A sometimes difficult paperback, but nonetheless quite interesting treatment of values, freedom, and man's purpose in relation to scientific fields.

Smith, Huston. *The Religions of Man.* New York: Harper and Row, 1965, Perennial Library edition. A remarkable and beautifully written introduction to the major religions, it is especially good for a beginning taste of Eastern thought, although seen through the eyes of a Westerner.

Stern, Karl. *Pillar of Fire.* Garden City, New York: Doubleday Image, 1965. Just one of many brilliant autobiographies that might be read. A Jewish-Catholic psychiatrist's relating of his early life as a materialist, Zionist, Communist, exile, and convert. He also wrote the Third Revolution, treating of the importance and influence of Freud.

Chapter Two

The Drive To Understand

I am aware of a world, spread out in space endlessly, and in time becoming and become, without end. I am aware of it; that means, first of all, I discover it immediately, intuitively, I experience it. Through sight, touch, hearing, etc., in different ways of sensory perception, corporeal things somehow spatially distributed are for me simply there in verbal or figurative senses "present", whether or not I pay them special attention by busying myself with them, considering, thinking, feeling, willing. Animal beings also, perhaps men, are immediately there for me; I look up, I see them, I hear them coming towards me, I grasp them by the hand; speaking with them, I understand immediately what they are sensing and thinking, the feelings that stir them, what they wish or will. They are present as realities in my field of intuition, even when I pay them no attention.[1]

Edmund Husserl

As I even begin to question, to philosophize, I am immediately aware of my presence to the world. I am already *in situation;* I am within the context from which my questioning emerges, a context that carries with it a demand to know who or what I am.

Upon recognition of this fact, I immediately hit upon a

method of investigation which is involved in the very act of questioning itself. Whatever I might eventually be able to say about myself or my context, one thing is already quite apparent. I want to *know;* that is why I am questioning. And although I can be fairly sure that questioning and wanting to know will involve a complexity of behavioral patterns, subjective states, and levels of action, I can nonetheless make an attempt at isolating various factors and data which are involved in my act of questioning.

What I *do* will tell me about who and what I am. And since I am the one who questions, who wants to know, a reflective analysis of my experience when I am questioning or knowing can lead me to a fuller understanding of my identity and my potentialities.

As we have seen, when I question I find myself already inserted into a situation of being present to the world and to myself. Consequently, when I try to understand what it means to know, I can see at least that involved in my knowing is a special kind of relationship with myself and with what is other than myself.[2] I am aware that I stand in relation to the world as a knower in a manifold number of ways. I can sense, feel, remember, affirm, and conceptualize it. In every case, however, if I know the *other,* I am in some way present to it (and it is present to me) in a unique yet complex experience. It is unique in that the object is both apart from me and a part of me; it is complex in that there are so many levels and types of awareness involved in it.

Before me "out there" is the other; and yet I am not only related to it as "out there." I also assimilate it in a unique way. The other remains what it is, where it is, separate from me, maintaining its own identity; nonetheless, when I come to know the other, it is also "of me" and going on "in me." When I see the other I do not change it, but some change does occur on my side of the relationship. The other is in me in a much different way than it is "out there" on its own. It seems that I have the image, or the shape, or the form of the other without having its extension, space, and quantity. In my act of knowing, then, I have some conditions which the known-object has; and yet I do not have all of its conditions. I have its signification, but not its material, extensional existence.

As a result, the union involved in knowing is quite different from a sheer spatial or macro-physical union. It is not like two objects tied or stuck together, not a union of blending, mixing, or physical assimilation (like eating something). From one point of view, I have come to be the other without being turned into it, and it has become part of me without losing anything of itself. I go on being what I was and the thing goes on being what it was; yet in some new way it is mine.

This description of what takes place in a knowledge situation can be summarized by the term "intentionality" (the knowledge-relationship of an object to a subject) or by the term "intentional union," in which an object exists in the knower under different conditions (in a different way) than it normally exists on its own. The object has meaning for me; it carries a signification. My knowledge is a transparent sign of the other.

The Level of Immediacy: Sense Knowledge

In knowing, I am present to the other. Experientially, I am aware of this phenomenon as a unified act even though the levels of my cognitive involvement are richly complex. This seems evident when I make myself aware of the quite different, and perhaps irreducible, factors involved in various acts of knowing. The total experience of being present to a particular person is couched in the complexity of alternating modes which complement and modify each other. The person before me becomes *of* me through signs, cues, immediate colors and sounds as well as through memories, affirmations, judgments, and comparisons.

Nonetheless, some differentiation between these various modes of knowing can, upon reflection, be made. In an admittedly somewhat artificial way, I can isolate a type of cognition which occurs in a most primitive and immediate way, although I might never experience it precisely in such an isolated and primal way. This primitive level of knowing occurs when I am present to the other under the rubrics of distinct and immediate cues to which I have access through the receptivity of external sense organs. Sounds, colors, odors, and textures have an obsessive immediacy in their presence to me insofar as I as hearer, seer, smeller, and toucher have an inescapable preoccupation with those very cognitive cues. I either see the color or I do not see it. To this extent, if I were able to be present to the world *only* on this level, my knowing of it could not escape the bondage of environment and immediate cues.

To call this level of knowing obsessive and primitive, nonetheless, is not to denigrate it. Rather it is to be made aware of its immense power and critical importance, not only for other modes of knowing, but for survival itself. Moreover, even on this primal level of presence, the knower breaks out in cognitive union with the other. Smell, touch, color, sound, and taste are not only cues. They are also *signs* of the other through which a union occurs in a way quite different from normal extensional and physical unions. Immediately and in a primal way, the person before me is in me in a different way than it is out there.

If our description thus far is correct, external sense knowledge forms a composite activity. The first aspect involves the characteristics of (a) environmental bondage and immediacy—the object sensed must be here and now present; (b) the medium by which the object is present to me has distinct material factors—sound waves, light waves or corpuscles, chemical reactions in the taste buds, etc.; (c) there is something of an obsessive dependence upon a particularized, concrete cue; (d) there is an external sense organ which serves as the receptor of the immediate data.

The second aspect of the composite act of sensation indicates that to some degree, even in this most primitive act of knowing, there is a release from environmental bondage—at least to the extent that a cognitive union does take place. The characteristics of this union are: (a) the fact that there is *signification,* a here-and-now immediate meaning, for the knower; (b) and the fact that there is a special union with the object known, which is not reducible to normal macro-physical unions of material assimilation, contiguity, or extensional continuity. The external organ itself could not account for these characteristics, nor can it account for the power of knowing on this level. Sensation, consequently, is the composite activity of the organ and the power. In my sensing of an object, I know not only by reason of the external organic receptor, but also through my own power to grasp meaning-for-me-here-and-now with respect to the sensed-cues I am receiving. Such is a descriptive analysis of *external sensation*.

There seems to be another way of sense knowledge, however, which shares in the characteristics of external sensation although it involves activities that cannot be achieved by the external organ-receptor. It is knowledge which is yet limited in its environmental and historical bondage and in its functioning through particular and concrete sense-cues. There are probably many distinguishable operations which occur on this level, but we can enumerate rather easily at least four:

1. I can *sense* that I am seeing, hearing, touching, etc. This is a type of awareness that is not reflective or deliberative. Rather it is an immediate sensory awareness of the environment. In this type of sensing, I can *unify* the various particular external sensations of an object and know sensorially the totally sensed object, e.g. the other as colored-sounding-touched all together. In order to get a total sense impression of all these external sensations, I must have the ability to sense which goes beyond each individual external sense-power. (The eye certainly cannot unify sound and smell into one image, nor can my eye distinguish them.) This power to unite particular sense images into one total sensed image, to combine sensations and to distinguish between them, we can call the *unifying sense power*. It manifests the same dual characteristics as external sensation, but its action and mode of knowing the object differ from the action and mode of knowing proper to external sensation. In the case of this type of sense knowledge, the organ is not external. Rather, as data from psychology, biology, and medical investigations point out, it seems clear that sections of the brain's cortex serve as the organ.

2. I can sense past images and cues which are quite particular, concrete, and immediate. Since the object is not externally present to me here and now, it is certainly not effected by an external organ. It is the brain again, in its bondage to historicity of past cues and images, that serves as the organ of sense-memory sensation. Dual characteristics are again present: environmental and historical bondage and the presence of a cognitive union.

26

3. I am also able to construct new sense images in combination or association with old ones. I can imagine sensorially something which I have never seen, like a centaur. Animals seem able to construct new sense images by associating old images or joining two different images within the environment—for example, apes putting two poles together to reach food which could not be obtained if the poles were used separately. This can be called *sense imagination*, involving again an organ-power, and having the dual characteristics of cognitive bondage and cognitive presence.

4. Finally, there seems to be (among others) another sense power in which I can sense an object as good or bad, benign or threatening, for me here and now in an immediate and concrete way which does not involve deliberation or reflection. This has been termed the power of *sense estimation*.

Both internal and external sensation occur within the bondage of historical and environmental immediacy. They are contingent upon the functioning of an external or internal organ; they are tied to cues, specific concrete images; they are operational in a form of cognitive abruptness, compulsively dependent upon the sign cue of here-and-now or then-and-there singularity. Any name might be ascribed to these characteristics. Some have called it the "material" aspect of cognition, although this term and its opposite often carry undesirable connotations. In any descriptive term, however, a radical dependence upon and bondage to historical and environmental immediacy would seem operative.

To call sense knowledge primal does not necessarily imply a pejorative judgment. To characterize it in this way is not only to point out its limitations of historical and environmental bondage; it is also to be made aware of its primacy in the development of all cognition. We must recognize sense knowing both for its importance in dealing with the immediacy of survival and deficiency and also for the richness it brings to fully realized human behavior. Through sensation, not only is the world made immediately present to us, we are made immediate to the world. It is the only way anything can get in; it is the only way anything of us can get out.

We probably never experience sense knowledge in the precise way that we have been talking about it. There are always affective and emotional states entering into the composite human act, and even other kinds of knowledge, such as affirmations, judgments, and conceptualizations. Nonetheless, it does seem that infants know and learn on this level and that animals (as complex as their knowing processes may be) apparently learn through sophisticated internal and external sensation activities. Whatever we may say about sensation, however, we should remain open to new ways of describing and interpreting it, both in the context of man-made-information-receivers and infra-sensate beings which could have an even more primal form of "presence" to the other.[3]

The Level of Distance: Transcending Immediacy

In my basic experience as a questioner, it is quite clear to me that I have other levels of knowledge which do not have the limitations and characteristics of sense knowledge, both internal and external. When I am *present to myself as a knower,* reflecting on myself as I question, revising and challenging my answers, and making general conclusions which I try to communicate to other questioners, I have overwhelming evidence that different knowing factors and characteristics are involved here than are involved in sensation. When I do all of these things implied in being a questioner, I experience a freedom from the bondage of the immediate object, from specific cues, from particular sense-images in my memory, and from the immediacy of environment and historicity. To be "freed from the immediate" does not mean that I totally transcend the actual conditions of being spread out in space and time, nor does it imply a privileged and remote isolation from what might be immediately before me. Quite to the contrary, in being freed from obsessive bondage to the immediate, I can bring new richnesses to it by seeing myself in relation to it.

Moreover, there are ways in which I can disengage myself from the singularity of the here and now and from concrete demands of sense stimuli. Sensation is now presented not only as survival and deficiency knowledge, but it can also be experienced as an invitation to further cognitive involvement. In this mode of knowing I undergo and initiate experiences which transcend the quantifiable organic limitations of sense knowing. And if these actions are indeed *mine,* then there must be something about me and my way of knowing which liberates me from the encapsulation of environment and closed historicity. This, in turn, might indicate a cognitive freedom from the conditions of here-and-nowness and materiality.

To understand more deeply this mode of knowing which transcends sensation, however, we must take a closer look at some of those activities in trans-sensorial cognition. Upon such an analysis, we might be able to understand more fully what our potentialities as questioners and knowers really are.

1. *Language.* The first activity which I might hit upon is the formation of language—part of the very constitution of question-asking. So great is its saturation in our experience that we can easily take for granted what happens in language formation. What takes place is that a word becomes a sign over which I have control. In language a word is not just a sound-cue or representation of something else, nor is it merely an external stimulus to which I react for the sake of some reward connected with it. Its meaning is not in its sound or look; rather, it is in the significance that I ascribe to it by my affirmation. Thus, it is not the mere fact that we can apprehend sounds as signs or that we can use sounds as communicative cues. The point is that I can take *possession* of the sign precisely as a sign and affirm meanings precisely for their own sake. Not only can I say that one thing means another; what is more, I can say that a thing *is* (without relation to utility or reward), that it is of a certain kind sharing a communality of its kind.

Language, then, is the comprehension and communication of meaning and intelligibility, freeing me from the cult and the attractions of the particular sign-cue at hand, by which I am able to *mean* what I am saying. Such a phenomenon seems to be non-reducible to sense knowledge or to any power which is limited to the bondage of immediacy or cue-stimuli.

2. *Formation of Universals.* Closely related to language, and indispensable to it, is the formation of universal ideas or abstract concepts. When I form an idea like "humanity," not only can it not

be predicated of any particular man, but I am signifying a meaning without experiencing its concrete realization here and now. The meaning of a universal is *open to realization* in any number of particulars. Hence, no particular sense image can exhaust its meaning. Although "truth" and "beauty" can be realized in particular cases and although my intelligibility of these concepts is partially derivative from sensation, no particular sensation or image or cue can be adequate to the meaning I am affirming and apprehending in using the concepts. This is not arriving at a definition by a process of cognitive subtraction. It is a recognition of the other in terms of what it is. I not only arrive at common characteristics, but I know what it *means* to have communality of characteristics. This cognitive act transcends any sense image or combination of sense images. It involves a release from the immediacy or promise of the object-cue at hand. All of these factors are mutually exclusive with the conditions intrinsic to sensation. The power by which I arrive at universals is qualitatively different from the powers of sensation in that it transcends the immediate, the singularity or combination of cues, and the bondage of here and now signification.

3. *The Horizon of Knowledge.* What can I know? Is there any limitation to the objects which I might have for my knowing? When I reflect upon this, it seems that anything that actually *is* is subject to my possibility of knowing it. I can know the whole range of sensations, I can know objects which are beyond the range of sensations, I can know knowledge itself, values, goals, relationships, abstractions, non-material concepts, things. None of these "objects" of knowing can exhaust the potentiality I have for knowing. My hunger for knowledge, unlike a physical appetite, is insatiable. I can always learn and strive for more. My knowledge, by the very fact of my ability to question things yet another time, is unconditional in its operation and possibilities. The horizon of my knowing is not anything particular, specific, or quantifiably determined; it is being itself, and my affirmation and questioning of it is not qualified by any particular case of being. Cognitive desire is insatiable on this level. It cannot be "filled-up."

4. *Self-Reflection.* Finally and most importantly—because all

of the previous intellectual acts could not take place without it—I call my attention to the fact that I *can* call my attention to something. What I mean by this is the act of self-reflection. Even now as I read or write, I am fully present to myself, transparent to myself in the present act of knowing, knowing that I am knowing, reflecting on my very reflection. Not only do I achieve a distance from the demands of the immediate environment; I also achieve a distance from myself and am enabled to see myself *in relation to* my environment. I am not enslaved by that which is here and now before me. Consequently, the extension of my concerns is expanded beyond anything possible in sense knowledge. My environment and my history are no longer a system of chains and blinders and necessities. With my ability to reflect upon myself and achieve a cognitive distance, environment and historicity are transformed from closed compulsions to open invitations.

In self-reflection, I bend back perfectly upon myself in an act of knowledge. This has critically important implications about the nature of the power by which I am able to self-reflect. Primarily, that power must be non-extensional, non-quantitative, and non-material. Any localized, material, and extended thing cannot, by the very fact that it has material and extensional parts outside of parts, "turn back upon itself" or be present to itself. In a material thing, one part can turn back upon another part, or we can double it in half, but the totality cannot be present to or "bent back upon" itself as a totality. The eye, because of its organic conditions, cannot see itself seeing, nor can memory be present to itself as memory. But in the case of self-reflection, consciousness of consciousness or reflection upon self-reflection, this is the very thing that takes place. This makes possible the experience of transcending historical and environmental necessity.

It seems clear then, that the power by which I perform self-reflection, as well as the other activities mentioned previously, is a power which must be non-material, non-extensional, and non-reducible to sensation or any other sheerly material operation. Questioning, cognitive revolution, language, abstraction, and self-reflection are the activities by which we will operationally define human intelligence. To be able to do these things is the basis of man's openness and self-transcending.

The Unity of Knowledge and the Radical Openness of Man

After having analyzed various factors in our knowing processes, we should point out two very important things. Although
the intellect transcends the limitations of matter and the immediacy
of sense knowledge, and although in itself the intellect is immaterial, it is quite important to realize that as far as we can tell—in
the present human condition—the intellect does depend *extrinsically*
upon the proper functioning of the brain. This is clear from the
evidence of what brain damage does to the operations of the
intellect. Nonetheless, the other fact remains, that when the brain
is in healthy organic condition, the human cognitive activities
extend qualitatively beyond the causality of the brain itself. In
other words, the brain is certainly an extrinsic condition for the
intellect's functioning in the present situation; but its causality is
that of an instrumentality, rather than that of an agent.[4]

Second, we should be aware of the close relationship between
all of our modes of knowing. Not only is the brain an extrinsic
condition for intellection; the dynamism of the intellect also
spiritualizes and permeates all of our sense knowledge when we have
an experience as a total person. This is why apparent "sensations"
can have such a stunning total effect upon us—e.g., the sight of an
horizon, the sound of special harmonies. Moreover, our very
cognitive growth depends upon the "cross-fertilization" of the
various levels of knowledge. We cannot come to a knowledge of
"truth" until we have seen and experienced "truthful" things and
persons; we cannot come to the idea of "humanity" until we have
sensed individual men; we cannot reflect upon ourselves until we
have experienced ourselves sensorially. On the other hand, witness
the case of Helen Keller to see what horizons are opened to the
human person, once sense-knowledge has been invaded by the light
of meaning and intelligence.[5]

In connection with this point, it should be clear to us that we
have a close communality with the rest of the animal world. Our

internal and external sense knowledge is quite close to that of many species of animals. We know as they know. But the outstanding difference is that we are not enslaved by the limitations of sense knowledge alone. Animals, too, are capable of the "intentional" cognitive union in the broad sense. They, too, sense, remember, sense-imagine, sense-estimate, and unify sense data; but these cognitive activities are tied down by the very conditions of sense knowledge itself. Such knowledge can be quite developed and sophisticated, but there does not seem to be any evidence at hand that animals ever break out of mere sensorial sophistication into a new, qualitatively different range of experience and possibility.

Such a range of cognitive possibilities includes for me, as a human person, the openness to the entire world of objects, material or otherwise. I can break out of the present and the immediate needs of the present. I not only assimilate, I am even able to be brought out of myself into the world of values and other persons. I am able to see things and persons not only as instruments or immediate signs of future rewards but as valid, beautiful, true, and good in themselves—even without relation to me, my demands, or my needs. In this qualitatively different type of knowing, I am no longer enclosed upon myself and the tight little world of deficiencies and immediate-as-possible-fulfillments. I am freed for deliberation upon future courses of actions because I can reflect upon myself and my situation. I am able to acquiesce in beauty and respond to meaning and value, since I am open to ultimacy and to a questioning of the proximate. I am able to take possession of myself since I can achieve a distance from necessity. And all of this is why I have been driven to question in the first place. If I had been hopelessly tied down to the immediate, I never would have bothered questioning at all. It would have had no chance to "cross my mind."

These are the reasons why I am present to the world in a far different way than the animal seems to be present to the world.[6] My intellect, with the activities that it makes possible, is the basis not only of my freedom from immediacy but also of the drive to transcend myself. The intellect, freed from deficit needs and of its very nature relational to *the other,* drives me outside of myself in the very act of questioning who, what, and why I am. Its basic dynamism being toward *all* that can be known, the mind seeks to comprehend the world and to penetrate to the very meaning of its own drive to understand, question, and affirm. Not satisfied by any physical need being fulfilled, it continually drives me outside of myself into fuller comprehension of anything that is there to be known. The dynamism of the intellect is not interiorly directed. Its fundamental action is not to embrace, because its grasp is fundamentally insatiable. Rather the motion of the intellect is to take myself outside of myself, for me *to be embraced* by all that is to be known.

Thus the questions of identity and action are beginning to be answered. I am an animal; yet I transcend my animality, driven as I am by that very factor in my knowing processes which distinguishes me from the infra-human. Much of my knowledge is indeed like that of an animal—a knowledge based upon immediate needs to be displaced or communicated, sensed goods or threats, direct cues and responses. And yet—often when these needs are fulfilled (and sometimes even when they are not)—I find myself released from their binds and discover that I am subject to a much different type of demand, rooted in the very exigencies of intelligence: the demand to comprehend anything that might be comprehended, the demand to raise questions about myself, the demand to take hold of myself (and a consequent demand to eventually let go), and the demand to remain faithful to what I know I ought to be.

Human consciousness is never totally closed in upon itself. The very notion of intentionality is openness to the object, to the *other*, to the world. The very meaning of a self-conscious being is to be placed outside oneself, a directedness to that which consciousness itself is not. This would seem to indicate, although it cannot be proven, that there is no real chasm between the knower and the known. Consciousness constitutes and fulfills itself in consciousness of the *other*. Man's identity as a knower, consequently, entails a presence to the other not only in the mode of an assimilating "bringing in," but also—in his fullest actuation as a knower—an unfolding of "going out."

From our own experience we can verify this partially when we realize what the accumulation of experience, of layers of awareness, can do to the richness of consciousness and the knowing process itself. Thus, after seeing the active aspects of knowing, we become aware of the passivities involved. In the fullness of knowing, I do not "take." I am taken away. This encounter does not ultimately involve an appropriation of the known, but rather it is a self-transcendence of the knower. Knowledge is not so much power or grasping as it is freedom and openness to being. In understanding my drive to understand, I find that the world is not only *for me*; I am also—in my very identity as a questioner wanting to know—*for the world and open to it.*

HYMN OF THE UNIVERSE
Pierre Teilhard de Chardin[7]

A limpid sound rises amidst the silence;

A trail of pure color drifts through the glass;

A light glows for a moment in the depths of the eyes I love. . . .

Three things, tiny, fugitive: a song, a sunbeam, a glance. . . .

So at first I thought they had entered into me in order to remain there and be lost in me. On the contrary; they took possession of me, and bore me away.

For if this plaint of the air, this tinting of the light, this communication of a soul were so tenuous and so fleeting,

it was only that they might penetrate more deeply into my being, might pierce through to that final x depths where all the faculties of man are so closely bound together as to become a single point.

Through the sharp tips of the three arrows which had pierced me the world itself had invaded my being and had drawn me back into itself.

We imagine that in our sense perceptions external reality humbly presents itself to us in order to serve us, to help in the building up of our integrity.

But this is merely the surface of the mystery of knowledge; the deeper truth is that when the world reveals itself to us it draws us into itself; it causes us to flow outwards into something belonging to it, everywhere present in it and more perfect than it.

The man who is wholly taken up with the demands of everyday living or whose *sole* purpose is the outward appearances of things, seldom gains more than a glimpse, at best of this second phase in our sense perceptions, that is, in which the world, having entered into us, then withdraws from us and bears us away with it; He can have only a dim awareness of that aureole, thrilling and inundating our being, through which is disclosed to us at *every* point of contact the unique essence of the universe.

I AND THOU: MAN AS RELATIONAL
Martin Buber[8]

To man the world is twofold, in accordance with his twofold attitude.

The attitude of man is twofold, in accordance with the twofold nature of the primary words which he speaks.

The primary words are not isolated words, but combined words.

The one primary word is the combination *I-Thou*.

The other primary word is the combination *I-It;* wherein, without a change in the primary word, one of the words *He* and *She* can replace *It*.

Hence the *I* of man is also twofold.

For the *I* of the primary word *I-Thou* is a different *I* from that of the primary word *I-It*.

Primary words do not signify things, but they intimate relations.

Primary words do not describe something that might exist independently of them, but being spoken they bring about existence.

Primary words are spoken from the being.

If *Thou* is said, the *I* of the combination *I-Thou* is said along with it.

If *It* is said, the *I* of the combination *I-It* is said along with it.

The primary word *I-Thou* can only be spoken with the whole being.

The primary word *I-It* can never be spoken with the whole being.

There is no *I* taken in itself, but only the *I* of the primary word *I-Thou* and the *I* of the primary word *I-It*.

When a man says *I* he refers to one or other of these. The *I* to which he refers is present when he says *I*. Further, when he says *Thou* or *It,* the *I* of one of the two primary words is present .

The existence of *I* and the speaking of *I* are one and the same thing.

When a primary word is spoken the speaker enters the word and takes his stand in it.

The life of human beings is not passed in the sphere of transitive verbs alone. It does not exist in virtue of activities alone which have some *thing* for their object.

I perceive something. I am sensible of something. I imagine something. I will something. I feel something. I think something. The life of human beings does not consist of all this and the like alone.

This and the like together establish the realm of *It.*

But the realm of *Thou* has a different basis.

When *Thou* is spoken, the speaker has no thing for his object. For where there is a thing there is another thing. Every *It* is bounded by others; *It* exists only through being bounded by others. But when *Thou* is spoken, there is no thing. *Thou* has no bounds.

When *Thou* is spoken, the speaker has no *thing;* he has indeed nothing. But he takes his stand in relation.

1. Edmund Husserl, *Ideas,* tr. by W. R. Boyce Gibson (New York: Macmillan, 1952), p. 101. The first English edition of this work (originally written in German and published in 1913) appeared in 1932.

2. See "Phenomenology of Knowledge" in Luijpen's *Existential Phenomenology.* (Pittsburgh: Duquesne University Press, 1953) This chapter has further reflections on the experience of knowing with reference to the positions of Descartes, the empiricists, Sartre, and others.

Our own method in this chapter entails a combination of descriptive phenomenology and simple reflective analysis.

3. With respect to sense-knowledge, for a more thoroughgoing philosophical analysis from a Thomistic point of view, see Klubertanz's *The Philosophy of Human Nature* (New York: Appleton-Century-Crofts, 1953), chapters six and seven. Also in Donceel's *Philosophical Anthropology* (New York: Sheed and Ward, 1967), you can find a broader range of data more closely related to psychology.

4. In this connection there are some considerations worthy of thought. The question has often been posed, "How can we arrive at immaterial knowledge if all of our knowledge is based upon sense knowledge?" Only an immaterial cause could bring about an immaterial effect. Does the intellect already have its knowledge prior to sensation? Is it actually independent of and discontinuous with sensation? Does it impose its own categories on sensation? This problem has been explained in many ways, one of the most coherent of which seems to be Thomas Aquinas' notion of the *agent intellect.* It is suggested that the agent intellect (each man's own active intellectualizing power of affirmation) dematerializes by efficient causality the product of sensation (the sense phantasm which acts as an instrumental cause). This does clarify a bit the relation between

the brain as an extrinsic condition for intellectual knowledge and the intellect which is in itself intrinsically independent of the brain and any other material conditions.

5. Helen Keller, *The Story of My Life* (New York: Grosset, 1904). Now in a paperback edition.

·6. Before judgments are made about the quality of knowledge involved in animal cognition, all that is asked is that research and reading be done. Rather than make any a priori statements, let it rest that—if animals do the things that seem to be distinctive to man (knowing and loving the way that man does), then we must either redefine the meaning of man or accept the fact that animals indeed have all the potentialities that men have.

7. Pierre Teilhard de Chardin, *Hymn of the Universe* (New York: Harper and Row, 1961), p. 79. Copyright©1961 by Editions du Seuil. Copyright © 1965 in the English translations by William Collins Sons & Company, London, and Harper & Row, Inc., New York. By permission of William Collins Sons & Company, London, and of Harper & Row, Publishers, Incorporated, New York.

8. Martin Buber, *I and Thou,* translated by Ronald Gregor Smith (New York: Charles Scribner's Sons, 1958), pp. 3-4. Reprinted by permission of Charles Scribner's Sons and T. & T. Clark.

Buber, Martin. *I and Thou*. New York: Scribners, 1958. Good for reflection upon the relational character of knowledge, the implications of intentionality, and the effects of man's ways of knowing himself and the other. Quite difficult at times.

Donceel, J. F. *Philosophical Anthropology*. New York: Sheed and Ward, 1967. Excellent for up-to-date bibliographies concerned with the specifically psychological aspects of sense knowing and intellectual knowing. Mixture of Phenomenology and Thomist philosophy. The readings at the end of the chapters are recommended for their anthropological and psychological data on man.

Klubertanz, G. P. *The Philosophy of Human Nature*. New York: Appleton-Century-Crofts, Inc., 1953. Quite a scholarly and thorough-going Thomistic approach to man. A necessity for further philosophical study with rather good bibliography and brilliant analyses of the cognitive processes.

Luijpen, William. *Existential Phenomenology*. Pittsburgh: Duquesne University Press, 1963. Another textbook, but from a more European, more modern standpoint. Rather enjoyable reading, sometimes difficult. The bibliographies and references are good for introduction to Merleau-Ponty, Sartre, Marcel, and some Heidegger.

Maslow, Abraham. *Toward a Psychology of Being*. Princeton, N.J.: Van Nostrand Insight Books, 1962. This has been referred to previously. Some of the middle chapters are quite excellent, dealing with the differences between "deficit-knowledge" and "being-knowledge."

42

McLuhan, Marshall. *Understanding Media.* New York: McGraw-Hill, 1964. This paperback, along with *The Medium is the Message,* is worth reading for minimally shattering many of the cognitive prejudices. Every page holds about ten challenges.

Novak, Michael. *Belief and Unbelief.* New York: Macmillan, 1967, paperback edition. This book is concerned with the knowledge of the self and of God. Notion of intelligent subjectivity is rather thoroughly developed. The book serves as an introduction to the much more difficult (and important) thought of Bernard Lonergan and his book, *Insight.*

Polanyi, Michael. *Personal Knowledge.* New York: Harper Torchbooks, 1958. Difficult but rewarding from countless points of view, not the least of which is a patient elucidation of convicted and passionate cognition on every level of knowing, even the scientific.

Chapter Three

The Drive To Do
Something About It

What I really lack is to be clear in my mind what I am to do, not what I am to know, except insofar as a certain understanding must precede every action. The thing is to understand myself, to see what God wishes me to do; the thing is to find a truth which is true for me, to find the idea for which I can live and die . . . What good would it do me to be able to explain the meaning of Christianity if it had no deeper significance for me and my life.[1]

Kierkegaard

Whether it is Kierkegaard demanding meaning in his life, or the common man "wanting to do something with himself," man realizes that thinking is not enough, that knowledge without consequent action is sterile, that understanding is next to being useless if it is not followed through with a continuity in some self-project. Action without intelligence dissipates itself in futile energy; but thought without commitment dies of its own indecisiveness. I must do something with what I have, what I know; whether it is to love passionately, communicate in desperation, or build some edifice by which I try to validate my being here. Knowledge not only has its own dynamism to embrace and to be embraced; it is the very root of man's total dynamism as a person. I must not only think. I must *do* something about it.

Knowledge does not take place in a vacuum. Since it is relational of its very nature, knowledge puts me immediately in relation to the world of others and of things.

In this way, when consciously awake, I find myself at all times, and without my ever being able to change this, set in relation to a world which, through its constant changes, remains one and ever the same. It is continually "present" for me, and I myself am a member of it. Therefore the world is not there for me as a mere *world of facts and affairs,* but with the same immediacy, as *a world of values, a world of goods, a practical world.* Without further effort on my part I find the things before me furnished not only with the qualities that befit their positive nature, but with value-characters such as beautiful, ugly, agreeable, or disagreeable, pleasant or unpleasant, and so forth. Things in their immediacy stand there as *objects to be used,* the "table" with its "books," the "glass" to drink from, the "vase," the "piano," and so forth. These values and practicalities, they too belong to *the constitution* of the "actually *present*" objects as such, irrespective of my turning or not turning to consider them or indeed any other object.[2]

In these words Husserl tries to describe the experience that we have of knowledge as being the basis of our presence *and attitude* toward the world. I am aware that consequent upon my presence (knowing) to the world, I take an attitude toward the world-as-known-by-me, an attitude of emotion, desire, aversion, or any other affective state.

Although the actions of knowing and "tending" are always found close together, we are nonetheless able to see a clear difference between knowing a thing and having a tendency to or away from it—between cognition and appetite, between understanding and doing something about what one understands. This distinction is clearly evident in the actual formulation of the meaning of questioning—wanting to know. Likewise the distinction can be seen in the formulation of the basic philosophical questions: identity—knowledge of who and what I am, and action—wanting to do something about it.

Added to this is the consistent correlation of knowing and tending in all of our experience. It is clear to us that we cannot love or choose what we do not know. Actually, most of our human relationships are built upon such a correlation. The intensity of our knowledge of another person greatly enhances and increases (or decreases) our love of that person. Understanding can lead to greater love and respect, just as a lack of understanding can lead to "irrational" and tyrannical fear. So important is our knowledge of another person that when we say, "I don't love you," we often mean that we really don't know the person—or that we know him too well. We constantly appeal to the fact that knowledge modifies our culpability and freedom, that we did not *know* the other alternatives. Then there are the hundreds of times when we hear and say the equivalent to, "I didn't *know* the gun was loaded."

Moreover, all of this personal experience is substantiated by the human-social world around us. Advertising (they have to *know* the product before they can *buy* it), the penal system (various degrees of murder and homicide depending upon premeditation or ignorance), education (to make people aware of the options before them), as well as political campaigning, propaganda, brainwashing, and other forms of thought control all indicate that appetite, tendency, and choice follow upon knowledge. Thus when I ask the question, "What am I do to?" my actions, my choices, and my attitudes will all depend a great deal upon the knowledge of just who I am, of what my potentialities are, and of what the alternatives may be. I see, then, that not only is "wanting" different from knowing, but my wanting and my willing follow upon and are modified by my knowledge. *Appetite is based upon and follows cognition.*

The Levels of "Wanting": Sensorial and Intellectual

As we have already seen, we have different types of knowledge. It seems worthwhile and necessary to ask, therefore, if different levels of knowledge have different corresponding levels of "wanting" or tending. And if we look at our experience, such a correspondence seems to be the case.

I can know a steak sensorially—its color, its smell, remembering its taste—and I can want the steak precisely on this level. Certainly animals, who know objects on this level, exhibit appetite on this level. But I can also know a steak intellectually: it is a steak, it has certain intelligible characteristics with other objects like it, it will do certain things for me with respect to my health, etc.

I can know intellectually that a certain medication or treatment may save my life, even though I may experience a sensory aversion to it. I can want warmth. But I can also want equality or justice. I desire pleasant sensations, and I "desire" freedom or self-dignity. I can want a person for my own uses. I can also want to give myself to that person.

In all of these cases of "wanting," a good is presented to me by way of sense knowledge or intellectual knowledge, or a combination of both. On the level of sense appetite, I experience a tendency toward a sensorially-known good, manifesting all of the immediate and concrete and material characteristics of sense knowledge. On the level of intellectual appetite, I experience a tendency toward an intellectually known good, manifesting the characteristics of immateriality, openness, and transcendence that were found in intellectual knowledge. This tendency toward an intellectually known good is called the will. And to have a will, one must have an intellect.

After making these considerations, we should not be led to think that sense demands are always less important than intellectual demands—especially when it is a matter of eating to stay alive. Again, we are indeed animals, and this is fundamental to our identity as men. Yet again we do transcend our animality in our knowing and wanting; and to fail to do so, to fail in fulfilling our potentialities of transcendence, is to negate our identity. What is important in all of this is that I am a unity, an event which can know not only the immediate, but anything which is knowable; and I am consequently open not only to the here-and-now good but to all good.

It might be repeated here that a difficulty in all of our discussions concerning the various levels of knowing and tending is continually present. Since all of our operations are *of us* as total unities, it would be rare to find a case of one level of our experience (sheer sense or sheer intellect) working in isolation from the other levels. Nonetheless, the different levels are there. We definitely have experiences in which it is evident that we are doing things which

47

otherwise would be impossible on a strictly sense level of knowing and wanting. And similarly, we can see cases in our experience where we are operating on a rather primal level of immediate needs, deficit gratifications, and a definitely limited scope of fulfillment.

Love of the Other for His Own Sake

A good example of these "levels" of knowing and wanting is presented in the writings of Abraham Maslow. He uses the categories of "being-cognition, being-love, deficit-cognition, and deficit love." And although there are similarities between these categories and the various categories we have been using, we should be careful not to make a simple identification of them. This warning being made, however, a look at some of Maslow's insights will be helpful in understanding the full implications of the self-transcendence involved in human powers of knowing and loving.

We have already seen that we are not tied down by the demands of the here-and-now object and that we can seek for goods which are not exhausted by and reducible to sense knowledge and tendencies—no matter how sophisticated the sense operations may be. I am certainly aware of basic needs and deficiencies which I tend to almost of necessity—the needs of safety, warmth, acceptance, organic growth. But there also seems to be an area, as Maslow points out in *Toward a Psychology of Being*,[3] in which I find tendencies which are not based upon needs or immediate demands, but rather on the drive to fulfill my potentialities as a self-transcending event. Maslow calls the operations on this level "being-cognition" and "being-love."

Some of the characteristics of "Being-love" are interesting, in that they manifest from a psychologist's point of view some traits which seem to transcend not only "deficiency-love" but any type of wanting that might occur on the sensory level alone. Maslow maintains that man is capable of (and has something of a moral imperative to actualize) a love which is non-possessive—in other words, a tendency which is not based upon appropriation of the object known. This type of love is admiring rather than needing. It is a special tendency which is not based upon a wanting of the object for one's own self. It is a loving of the object simply because it is lovable, a wanting it to be just the way it is. Being-love is "beyond the shadow of a doubt, a richer, higher, more valuable subjective experience than deficiency-love."[4] As opposed to deficit needs which can easily be satiated, being-love is insatiable, seemingly having no particular object as its fulfillment, but just the delighting in the good of the object—without having to grab it or tamper with it. When applied to persons, Maslow says, "Being-lovers are more independent of each other, more autonomous, less jealous, less threatened, less needful, more individual, more disinterested, but also simultaneously more eager to help the other toward self-actualization, more proud of his triumphs, more altruistic, generous, and fostering."[5]

The point is not only that man can do things like those mentioned above; it is more significantly maintained that an individual is more himself, more integrated, and more fulfilled when he is doing them. Notice that here, as we found in the case of the true dynamism of intellectual knowledge, the movement of this type of love is *out from* the subject. Its fullest exercise and meaning are attained not in appropriation but in transcending to the other. Again, man's identity in its deepest meaning seems to be ontologically directed toward the other, toward the unconditionally true, the unqualified good.

Being-love, logically enough, Maslow says, is based upon being-cognition (appetite follows cognition) in which the object is seen as a whole, a unit, detached from relations, from personal utility. The other is seen in himself, unique, irreplaceable, as the sole member of his class. And since I am able to know the other in this way, I am able to love him similarly. I can love the other for himself, because he is himself, because he is lovable.

Involved in all of this is the ability of man to see and to respond to values which are not found sensorially and are not limited to the conditions of immediate sense reward, gratification, or stimulation from the object-to-be-grasped-here-and-now-for-me. The experiences of being-love and being-cognition exhibit "wholeness, perfection, completion, justice, beauty, just-rightness, aliveness, autonomy, richness, simplicity, goodness, oughtness, uniqueness, effortlessness, truth, honesty, playfulness, joy, purity, and independence."[6]Here Maslow gives us an amazing categorization of human experiences which cannot be reduced to the level of sheer physicality, concreteness, and material need. Not only is the person living on a higher level, but the horizon of possibilities that he sees in the world is broadened extensively. "The person at the peak experience is godlike not only in the senses that I [Maslow] have touched upon already but in certain other ways as well, particularly in the complete, loving, uncondemning, compassionate, and perhaps amused acceptance of the world and the person."[7]

Abraham Maslow, then, seems to reinforce the notion of man's identity toward which we have been tending. Man at his peak is autonomous yet ego-transcending, free yet captured, as it were, by the value of the other, unified yet aware of his complexity. On his highest cognitive and appetitive levels, man is open to the world of values, the good, the true. Again here we see, as we noted in the citation from Teilhard concerning knowledge, that love is precisely not appropriating and grasping the world of objects and persons, but is rather being grasped and embraced by the world of people and things to which we are radically open.

Perhaps this is still another way of looking at the difference between animals and men. The animal can never break out of itself and the immediacy of the environment or object at hand. On the other side we have man, who not only in his formation of language and concepts but also in the very dynamism of his human powers to know and love is fulfilled by the "losing" or "being brought of himself." Man's very identity includes being open to the other. He can know not merely particular objects, but he can know and affirm all that is knowable. He can love or tend not only to what is sensorially immediate to him or necessarily innate in him, but he can tend to the good itself—precisely because it is good—without qualification of his own needs and demands.

Man's central identity is certainly as a center of activities and an autonomous self. But that identity is fulfilled only in the *centrifugal* action of cognitive and appetitive openness to the horizon of all that is good and true as seen in the world of persons and things.

At this point we might easily begin a discussion of the implications involved with our potentialities to know and to love. The distance achieved in self-knowledge and liberation from immediate demands will bring us to a consideration of human freedom and self-possession. We will also be interested in what happens when the dynamisms of human knowing and loving are directed to another human being.

But before doing this, we ought to look a bit more closely at the answers we have found with respect to the question of identity. In seeking to find out "who I am," we tried to understand what was involved in the very asking of the question in the first place. And since *wanting to know* is the foundation of questioning itself, we attempted to understand the ways and levels of knowing and wanting that we find in our experience. Having made the investigation, we ought to consider how all of these findings fit together.

The Unity of Human Powers in the Total Person

In the range of knowing, we found two qualitatively different levels of being present to the world: one level quite immediate and directly tied down to cues, specific objects, or potential reward; and the other level expansive enough to be open to all that can be known, liberated from sense immediacy, and capable of possibilities beyond the grasp of senses.

In the range of tending, we saw the correlative levels of sense appetite and intellectual appetite (the will). This latter, possessing a dynamism quite similar to intellectual knowledge upon which it is based, was discovered to be most fully-functioning not when it was directed to the fulfillment of needs or immediate desires, but when it wanted the object to be just the way it is, because it is good and thereby worthy of my love.

It follows, then, that I am the type of event that can do these things, knowing and loving, in the particular ways mentioned above. All of these powers or potentialities are distinct from one another because they have distinctly different operations, different terms of their activities, different formal objects. Moreover, it also seems that each of these powers is distinct from me and my "to be," or the total-me as an existing thing on its own. I am the same person, even if I am not manifesting the activity of knowing or exercising my ability to love at this particular time. In other words, my identity as a self and as a man is different from my actions and operations. And although my activities (as observed) tell me about and help me discover my potentialities, and thereby help me to understand what I am (my nature), nevertheless, these activities *are not* me. Quite to the contrary, it is the fact that I am *what I am* which enables me to do these actions, not *vice versa*. We might look at this diagrammatically. First, on the level of discovery and investigation, we go from:

ACTIVITIES to POTENTIALITIES to NATURE

But on the level of who I am and why I am able to do what I do, the causality is just the opposite:

I am a NATURE with POTENTIALITIES for ACTIVITIES

Those powers and potentialities for knowing and loving which I have discovered in myself and other men and which are not shared by any other "nature" are the very potentialities which distinguish me as a man and separate me from "non-men." If I am a man, I must have these potentialities; if I do not have these potentialities which are proper to humans, there is no reason for saying that I am a man. Human nature, then, in this sense, is the basis of why I am able to do properly human activities, the dynamic principle of human operations.

All of this is merely to say that we can know the *what* or nature of a thing by looking at and investigating its distinctive activities and potentialities—its "proper powers." We know the essence or nature of a thing by first observing what it does; if a thing had no activities, we could not know or say anything about it. And this is precisely what we did in our own case as questioners. We first asked, "What am I doing when I question; what is involved in questioning, in wanting to know?" From this starting point we discovered more about our potentialities as knowers, wanters, questioners, sighted the specific differences between sheer animal knowing and human knowing, and drew some conclusions about what it means to be a human with specific human potentialities.

In conclusion, then, it seems rather important to note again that we can have the power or potentiality to do human things even though the activity is not manifestly functioning. For example, sleeping, although it apparently prevents the activity of choosing or loving, does not make me a non-man or take away my capability to choose or to love. The same is true in the case of a little baby. Maturation is a necessary condition for the functioning of its powers to know and love. But the potentialities are there in the child. Time does not bestow the potentiality; the baby has it already—otherwise we would have little reason for the baby to turn out a man rather than a monkey. The material conditions of maturation are just not there. Similarly, the absence of the material conditions does not divest a drunk of his humanity; they merely prevent proper functioning.

Finally, we might say, then: my substantial identity, or the totality that is me-on-my-own, is the dynamic total reality operating through my powers, which are precisely those powers which make me this particular kind of being. My human powers, and the unique way in which they are developed or actualized, are what make me different and unique as a particular man, and they are the basis of my community with and transcendence from sheer animality.

The Soul: Radical Basis of Unity in a Person

The discussion of human potentialities, powers, and activities leads us to a realization of the complexity in my identity. I am one who sees, who asks, who listens, who hurts, who blushes, who loves. I do biological things, vegetative things, animal things, and supra-animal things; and I am aware of them all. I am like a stone, a flower, a monkey; and yet I am more. Does all of this mean that I am basically *many* in my identity; or am I really two beings—an animal thing and a rational thing? Does my complexity mean that I am not *one*? Or from a chemical point of view, am I just a conglomeration of elements structurally working together?

In a response to these questions which I pose to myself, my first appeal is to the direct experience of myself as the perduring subject—I who am doing all of these things. I know myself as myself; you step on my toe and you step on me; you hurt any part of me and you are hurting me, the subject of these hurts. Moreover, I am aware of myself as distinct and apart from others. My primary experience is that I am a unity, a living-one-on-my-own. I am aware that it is not a unity of perfect simplicity, because I have parts, different actions, different drives. Nor am I a unity of mere structure, like a pile of cemented bricks; or a simple dynamic unity in the way that all of the parts of a clock or an automobile work together. Although a unity of structure and dynamism is part of my experience as one being, my experience entails much more—that is the fact that I work within myself to perfect myself and actualize myself, that I have one basic unity of purpose—an internal drive for self-actualization.

The most striking evidence is that all of my actions and my parts are primarily and directly ordered together for the intrinsic good of myself as a whole. As Carl Rogers has said, "The organism has *one basic tendency* and striving—to actualize, maintain, and enhance the experiencing organism."[8] All of my living, feeling, and thinking actions manifest a unity in me of operating for-me-perfecting-and-actualizing myself. There is one end and finality, the good of the whole; and this one end and goal demands one unified organizing and finalizing principle of all these operations. Historically this principle (on the *living* level) has been called the soul. The soul, which is precisely the unifying principle of a living thing's activities, makes the difference between a living and a non-living thing. In the case of myself, a man, it is this principle (the human soul) of all my activities as a total man that makes me different from a non-man.[9] And so that by which I am precisely a human, capable of human activities, knowing and loving, is the human soul. It is the here-and-now existential reason why I am *this* type rather than another type with different operations and

54

potentialities. And it is the soul which is the very principle unifying all of my activities for the same finality of self-actualization—not only growth, self-repair, reproduction, and nutrition (specifically "living" activities) but also all my levels of knowing and loving as a human person.

We will make some further considerations about the meaning of "soul" in later chapters; but now, having seen the complexity and unity involved in our identity as a questioner, knower, and lover, we will look first at some of the more immediate implications of what our identity means to us in the realm of action—specifically human actions of free self-possession and free self-gift.

SOME BASIC PROPOSITIONS OF A GROWTH AND SELF-ACTUALIZATION PSYCHOLOGY

Abraham Maslow[10]

When the philosophy of man (his nature, his goals, his potentialities, his fulfillment) changes, then everything changes, not only the philosophy of politics, of economics, of ethics and values, of interpersonal relations and of history itself, but also the philosophy of education, of psychotherapy and of personal growth, the theory of how to help men become what they can and deeply need to become.

We are now in the middle of such a change in the conception of man's capacities, potentialities and goals. A new vision is emerging of the possibilities of man and of his destiny, and its implications are many, not only for our conceptions of education, but also for science, politics, literature, economics, religion, and even our conceptions of the non-human world.

I think it is now possible to begin to delineate this view of human nature as a total, single, comprehensive system of psychology even though much of it has arisen as a reaction *against* the limitations (as philosophies of human nature) of the two most comprehensive psychologies now available—behaviorism (or associationism) and classical, Freudian psychoanalysis. Finding a single label for it is still a difficult task, perhaps a premature one. In the past I have called it the "holistic-dynamic" psychology to express my conviction about its major roots. Some have called it "organismic" following Goldstein. Sutich and others are calling it the Self-psychology or Humanistic psychology. We shall see. My own guess is that, in a few decades, if it remains suitably eclectic and comprehensive, it will be called simply "psychology."

I think I can be of most service by speaking primarily for myself and out of my own work rather than as an "official" delegate of this large group of thinkers, even though I am sure that the areas of agreement among them are very large. Because of the limited space I have, I will present here only some of the major propositions of this point of view. I should warn you that at many points I am way out ahead of the data. Some of these propositions are more based on private conviction than on publicly demonstrated facts. However, they are all in principle confirmable or disconfirmable.

1. We have, each one of us, an essential inner nature which is instinctoid, intrinsic, given, "natural," i.e., with an appreciable hereditary determinant, and which tends strongly to persist. . . .

It makes sense to speak here of the hereditary, constitutional and very early acquired roots of the *individual* self, even though the biological determination of self is only partial, and far too complex to describe simply. In any case, this is "raw material" rather than finished product, to be reacted to by the person, by his significant others, by his environment, etc.

I include in this essential inner nature instinctoid basic needs, capacities, talents, anatomical equipment, physiological or temperamental balances, prenatal and natal injuries, and traumata to the neonate. This inner core shows itself as natural inclinations, propensities or inner bent. Whether defense and coping mechanisms, "style of life," and other characterological traits, all shaped in the first few years of life, should be included is still a matter for discussion. This raw material very quickly starts growing into a self as it meets the world outside and begins to have transaction with it.

2. These are potentialities, not final actualizations. Therefore they have a life history and must be seen developmentally. They are actualized, shaped or stifled mostly (but not altogether) by extra-psychic determinants (culture, family, environment, learning, etc.). Very early in life these goalless urges and tendencies become attached to objects ("sentiments") by canalization, but also by arbitrarily learned associations.

3. This inner core, even though it is biologically based and "instinctoid," is weak in certain senses rather than strong. It is easily overcome, suppressed or repressed. It may even be killed off permanently. Humans no longer have instincts in the animal sense,

powerful, unmistakable inner voices which tell them unequivocally what to do, when, where, how, and with whom. All that we have left are instinct-remnants. And furthermore, these are weak, subtle, and delicate, very easily drowned out by learning, by cultural expectations, by fear, by disapproval, etc. They are *hard* to know, rather than easy. Authentic selfhood can be defined in part as being able to hear these impulse-voices within oneself, i.e., to know what one really wants or doesn't want, what one is fit for and what one is *not* fit for, etc. It appears that there are wide individual differences in the strength of these impulse-voices.

4. Each person's inner nature has some characteristics which all other selves have (species-wide) and some which are unique to the person (idiosyncratic). The need for love characterizes every human being that is born (although it can disappear later under certain circumstances). Musical genius however is given to very few, and these differ markedly from each other in style, e.g., Mozart and Debussy.

5. It is possible to study this inner nature scientifically and objectively (that is, with the right kind of "science") and to discover what it is like (*discover*—not invent or construct). It is also possible to do this subjectively, by inner search and by psychotherapy, and the two enterprises supplement and support each other. An expanded humanistic philosophy of science must include these experiential techniques.

6. Many aspects of this inner, deeper nature are either (a) actively repressed, as Freud has described, because they are feared or disaproved of or are ego-alien, or (b) "forgotten" (neglected, unused, overlooked, unverbalized or suppressed), as Schnachtel has described. Much of the inner, deeper nature is therefore unconscious. This can be true not only for impulses (drives, instincts, needs) as Freud has stressed, but also for capacities, emotions, judgments, attitudes, definitions, perceptions, etc. Active repression takes effort and uses up energy. There are many specific techniques of maintaining active unconsciousness, such as denial,

projection, reaction-formation, etc. However, repression does not kill what is repressed. The repressed remains as one active determinant of thought and behavior.

Both active and passive repressions seem to begin early in life, mostly as a response to parental and cultural disapprovals.

However, there is some clinical evidence that repression may arise also from intra-psychic, extra-cultural sources in the young child, or at puberty, i.e., out of fear of being overwhelmed by its own impulses, of becoming disintegrated, of "falling apart," exploding, etc. It is theoretically possible that the child may spontaneously form attitudes of fear and disapproval toward its own impulses and may then defend himself against them in various ways. Society need not be the only repressing force, if this is true. There may also be intra-psychic repressing and controlling forces. These we may call "intrinsic counter-cathexes."

It is best to distinguish unconscious drives and needs from unconscious ways of cognizing because the latter are often easier to bring to consciousness and therefore to modify. Primary process cognition (Freud) or archaic thinking (Jung) is more recoverable by, e.g., creative art education, dance education, and other non-verbal educational techniques.

7. Even though "weak," this inner nature rarely disappears or dies, in the usual person, in the U.S. (such disappearance or dying is possible early in the life history, however). It persists underground, unconsciously, even though denied and repressed. Like the voice of the intellect (which is part of it), it speaks softly but it *will* be heard, even if in a distorted form. That is, it has a dynamic force of its own, pressing always for open uninhibited expression. Effort must be used in its suppression or repression from which fatigue can result. This force is one main aspect of the "will to health," the urge to grow, the pressure to self-actualization, the quest for one's identity. It is this that makes psychotherapy, education and self-improvement possible in principle.

8. However, this inner core, or self, grows into adulthood only partly by (objective or subjective) discovery, uncovering and

acceptance of what is "there" beforehand. Partly it is also a creation of the person himself. Life is a continual series of choices for the individual in which a main determinant of choice is the person as he already is (including his goals for ego-strength or "will power," etc.). We can no longer think of the person as "fully determined" where this phrase implies "determined only by forces external to the person." The person, insofar as he *is* a real person, is his own main determinant. Every person is, in part, "his own project" and makes himself.

9. If this essential core (inner nature) of the person is frustrated, denied or suppressed, sickness results, sometimes in obvious forms, sometimes in subtle and devious forms, sometimes immediately, sometimes later. These psychological illnesses include many more than those listed by the American Psychiatric Association. For instance, the classical disorders and disturbances are now seen as far more important for the fate of the world than the classical neuroses or even the psychoses. From this new point of view, new kinds of illness are most dangerous, e.g., "the diminished or stunted person," i.e., the loss of any of the defining characteristics of humanness, or personhood, the failure to grow to one's potential, valuelessness, etc.

That is, general-illness of the personality is seen as any falling short of growth, or of self-actualization, or full-humanness. And the main source of illness (although not the only one) is seen as frustrations (of the basic needs, of the B-values, of idiosyncratic potentials, of expression of the self, and of the tendency of the person to grow in his own style and at his own pace) especially in the early years of life. That is, frustration of the basic needs is not the only source of illness or of human diminution.

1. Soren Kierkegaard, *Journals,* tr. by Alexander Dru (New York: Harper Torchbooks, 1959), p. 44.

2. Edmund Husserl, *Ideas* (New York: Macmillan, 1952), p. 103.

3. Abraham Maslow, *Toward a Psychology of Being* (Princeton N. J.: Insight, Van Nostrand, 1962).

4. *Ibid.,* p. 40

5. *Ibid.*

6. *Ibid.,* p. 78.

7. *Ibid.,* p. 87.

8. See the article by Carl Rogers, "A Humanistic Conception of Man," from *Science and Human Affairs,* ed. by Richard Farson (Palo Alto: Science and Behavior Books, Inc., 1965).

"It has been stressed that the human organism is directional, but perhaps this tendency can be described with more precision. The human individual appears to move, inherently, toward the development of all its capacities in ways which serve to maintain or enhance the organism . . . It involves movement toward new experience for its own sake . . . It is a trend toward autonomy, the increased control of events, and away from heteronomy, the control *by* events." pp. 22-23 of reprint.

9. "For [Saint] Thomas, there are two significant characteristics of a living being: the tendency to actualize potentialities from within, and the tendency of a partially actualized potentiality toward further actualization. And for him this is not determined wholly by random contact with environment or mere need to maintain the status quo, but by the whole scope of our unrealized capacities; by man's nature, if you will, but an open-end nature endowed with objectively unlimited capacities and goals as broad and deep as all being." From James E. Royce, *Man and His Nature* (New York: McGraw-Hill, 1961), pp. 233-4. Compare this quote in conjunction with the Rogers article cited above. Quite interesting

similarities will be seen.

10. Abraham Maslow, *Toward a Psychology of Being* (2nd ed.; Princeton: Van Nostrand Insight Books, 1962), pp. 189-194. Reprinted by permission of D. Van Nostrand Company.

Brown, Norman O. *Life Against Death*. New York: Vintage, 1959. This is a mytho—poetic, psychoanalytic interpretation of human history and human desire. A broad, well-written synthesis, it might be read with Herbert Marcuse's *One-Dimensional Man*, another Freudian approach to man in the context of freedom and a closed cultural structure.

Castell, Alburey. *The Self in Philosophy*. New York: Macmillan, 1965. This is a brief but well-developed and well-argued treatment of the meaning of the self as the central unifying agency of human action. It is worth careful reading.

Hazo, Robert G. *The Idea of Love*. New York: Praeger, 1967. Hazo's work is part of the "Concepts in Western Thought" series. It develops the whole notion of appetite, tendency, love, and eros both historically and thematically.

Lawrence, Nathaniel and O'Connor, Daniel, ed. *Readings in Existential Phenomenology*. New Jersey: Prentice-Hall, 1967. A valuable book of extended selections covering many areas, including embodiement, emotion, affectivity, and volition.

May, Rollo. *Love and Will*. New York: Norton, 1969. A very readable (and perhaps soon-to-be influential) treatment of human affectivity, passion, and sexuality in the context of contemporary society.

Rubinoff, Lionel. *The Pornography of Power*. New York: Ballantine, 1969. This is a study of man in the context of irrationalism, violence, and the drive for power; it attempts to resolve these problems through an appeal to creative imagination. It could be read with a more specific (and much less speculative) book on aggression, *A Sign For Cain* by Fredric Wertham.

Chapter Four

Human Freedom

"Well, right now," said Castle. He picked up a book of matches. "I'm free to hold or drop these matches."

"You will, of course, do one or the other," said Frazier. "Linguistically or logically there seem to be two possibilities, but I submit that there's only one in fact. The determining forces may be subtle but they are inexorable. I suggest that as an orderly person you will probably hold—ah! you drop them! Well, you see, that's all part of your behavior with respect to me. You couldn't resist the temptation to prove me wrong. It was all lawful. You had no choice. The deciding factor entered rather late, and naturally you couldn't foresee the result when you first held them up. There was no strong likelihood that you would act in either direction, and so you said you were free."[1]

B. F. Skinner

Man is nothing else but that which he makes of himself. That is the first principle of existentialism . . . If, however, it is true that existence is prior to essence, man is responsible for what he is. Thus the first effect of existentialism is that it puts every man in possession of himself as he is, and places the entire responsibility for his existence squarely upon his own shoulders.[2]

Jean-Paul Sartre

> *Life is a continual series of choices for the individual in which a main determinant of choice is the person as he already is (including his goals for himself, his courage or fear, his feeling of responsibility, his ego-strength or "will power," etc.). We can no longer think of the person as "fully determined" where this phase implies "determined only by forces external to the person." The person, insofar as he is a real person, is his own main determinant. Every person is, in part, "his own project" and makes himself.*[3]
>
> Abraham Maslow

All men seem to be at least experientially aware of freedom in choice. The experience is so primary, in fact, that it is difficult to conceive oneself operating as if there were no freedom at all. Data from literature, history, and personal communication present manifold testimony not only to freedom, but to the ambiguity, the deliberation, the irrevocability, and even the terror of it. It has often been maintained that this universal experience of freedom provides the greatest proof for its own existence.

Before I place an act, I am aware that I can or cannot do it, that I have various alternatives before me which represent various limited aspects of what might be good for me here and now or in the long run. Even during the placement of the act itself, I can make myself aware of its dependence upon *my* continuing the act. And after the action is completed, I am aware that I did it, that it is *mine*—part of me, an extension of myself, a self-project, a creation. This final awareness often brings with it either a feeling of well being, accomplishment, or guilt and failure.

It is precisely this primary, universal experience, however, which has been called into question by philosophers, theologians, psychologists, and even historians. The three quotations introducing this chapter represent at least some of the positions taken.

B. F. Skinner, an extremely influential behavioral psychologist from Harvard, seems to affirm that man is not free because a) all present behavior is controlled by previous behavior, including the entire network of environmental, psychological, and educational stimuli which have shaped our present characters and personalities, and b) all behavior (even the dropping of a book of matches) has motivational causes which are necessitating causes. We might summarize this basically by saying: *man is determined by his historicity*.

Quite to the contrary of Skinner, Jean-Paul Sartre's position seems to be one of absolute indeterminism or total freedom. In Sartre's view man actually has no history. The individual has only his future project which he makes entirely of himself and for which he alone is responsible. Man is so free, so indeterminate, that he cannot even be defined.

Abraham Maslow offers something of a compromise position. Man cannot be reduced to his historicity, to his environment, to determinism; nor can man be totally divorced from them. To be a human person means a) to have potentialities which liberate him from blind necessity—to be able to know, question, and mould himself, and b) to be inserted into an environment and history which help him actualize these potentialities.

All three of these men will merit our further consideration, but before we begin to enter debate or controversy, we should first look reflectively at our own experience to see what important personal data should be accounted for within any theory that might be proposed.

Phenomenological Analysis of Reflection and Questioning

Involved in the very act of reflection which we are right now making in communicating and understanding, in Skinner's act of offering the hypothesis of determinism, in Sartre's formulation of absolute freedom, and in Maslow's middle course, is an important phenomenon of human behavior that is worthy of our consideration. In philosophical and scientific reflection we experience a *distance* from objects and demands which are presently before us. We are able to "hesitate" cognitionally by questioning the status quo. Skinner is at least not enslaved by his environment or by blind necessity to the extent that he cannot *question* that environment and formulate hypotheses about it and invite others to share his attitudes. He shares, with Sartre, Maslow, you, and me, the ability to question, to hesitate, to achieve a distance from immediate necessity.

Therefore at least the immediate objects before us and the immediate tasks at hand do not compel or force us. We have by our questioning achieved a distance from and a certain control over the immediate environment. Moreover, all of us share in the ability to question our historicity and our past: Skinner does this with the American values of competition and property accumulation; Sartre does it with traditional values of "natural law" and religious belief; we do it with the values of our country, our church, or our family. To this extent, we certainly are not enslaved by our past—or hopelessly determined by it.

All of this is to say that none of the objects, tasks, or values which I confront can exhaust the complexity of my desires and aspirations. None of them, on their own, can constrain me definitively or hinder me from making further considerations about the advisability of responding to them. Since—as we have already seen—I have the potentialities of knowing and wanting in ways that transcend the immediacy of any particular need, object, or satisfaction, by these very potentialities I achieve a distance from the demanding stimuli of things and I am able consequently to say something about *my* response. *Being able to say something about my response to stimuli, to environment, to values is the first point worth noting with respect to the distance involved in questioning and cognitive hesitation.*

A second important point is that I can reflect upon myself. To this extent, I acquire a distance from myself-as-one-immediately-concerned-with-the-present-stimulus. I can look at myself in relation to my present needs, my past experiences, my environmental heritage. Then, reflecting upon myself, and seeing myself in relation to all these things, I can act upon this knowledge. I can take myself in hand, you might say, and consider the horizons of who I am, what my potentialities are, and what I might want to make of myself. The second point, then, is that *with the distance I achieve from myself in self-reflection, I am able to achieve—at least to some extent—self possession and self determination.*

Distance from the immediate demands before me, distance in seeing myself as related to my own state-of-affairs: this is why questioning is possible for me in the first place, because in the distance of self-reflection I am able to take myself, my environment, my needs, and my values and say, "Wait a second—I do not have to do that." By the very act of calling something into question I am liberating myself from the chains of necessity. Questioning then—which we saw as the starting point of philosophy—implies some minimal self-possession. Seen in this way, questioning implies that the questioner is free. In the act of freedom which questioning is, I am able to ask who, what, and why I am. Only then will I be able to possess myself fully. And only when I can possess myself can I give myself to the life-project which I, in my philosophizing, have formulated. Thus questioning is not only the beginning of philosophy. It is also the initiation into the formulation of my own creative project which is my life—lived in fidelity to what I understand as my true identity.

To these factors in my experience which I have been talking about I will assign the name *freedom*. It entails:

a) achieving a distance in reflection from blind necessity with respect to external stimuli, environment, values, immediate objects, and present needs;

b) achieving a distance from myself in self-reflection whereby I am able to see myself in relation to present needs, past experiences, and future rewards; and whereby I am able to question these relationships;

c) achieving a possession of myself in reflecting upon who I am and what my potentialities might be—self-possession;

d) being able to say something about myself—self-determination.

All of this is not to claim that I am absolutely free. It is merely to say that I do this, that Sartre does this, that Skinner does this, that anyone who can question and reflect upon himself can do it.

Free Choice: A Metaphysical Analysis of the Will

One might well ask what the notions of distance, questioning, and self-reflection have to do with the more common notions of free choice. And although the concept of self-possession is most fundamental to our understanding of freedom, a discussion from an analytic point of view concerning the freedom of the will might be valuable here. Here we will try to understand more fully the meaning of the will as we have discussed it in the last chapter. We will try to investigate the nature of the dynamism involved when an act of the will is placed or when we choose something.

In the last chapter we saw that the will was an intellectual tendency, or a tendency toward an intellectually known good. It is different from sense appetite in that it is not "chained down" by the immediacy of the sensed object. (Note that the idea of distance is again operative here.) I know not only *this* object as good, but I know all objects, all subjects, all that *is,* as good in some respect—at least insofar as it exists. Anything then, because it can be seen as good, might be the object of my will—whether it is a good steak, a good person, a good feeling, or a good action. It is precisely because a thing or action can be seen as having good aspects that my will goes out to it or tends toward it. The very reason that I find myself having a tendency toward an object in the first place is because I sense it or know it as having good things about it. It is the "good" quality of the thing by which the will is drawn or moved.

We might say, then, that the will is naturally determined to seek the good; and if I were ever presented with an unmitigated, simple, unqualified good, my will would certainly be necessitated toward it. With this in mind—that all things are good in some way and that my will tends spontaneously toward them because they are somehow good—I recognize nevertheless that my "tending" is always concerned with an existential, real world in which goods are precisely limited, finite, conditioned, interrelated, and ordered to other goods. If I am about to undertake a course of action, it is often evident that a number of possibilities—all of which have good and bad points to recommend and discredit them—are presented to me as alternatives. Since none of these alternative "goods" can be called unconditional or simple goods, and since none of them can exhaust the total meaning of good in which they all participate, none of them can force my will to a necessary choice. This is our reasoning:

a) the will is a tendency toward an intellectually known good; thus it is precisely the "good" aspect of the object which attracts my will;

b) the only object which could necessitate my will would be a good that is unconditionally good in an unqualified sense;

c) in many of my choices, however, the goods from which I select as "the good for me in this decision" are all conditioned, limited, and qualified;

d) therefore freedom of choice can be operative in my behavior.

We might note that if there should be a case in which a particular good appeared to be absolute—due to a lack of knowledge or an excess of fear and emotion—then freedom of choice would be inoperable. Similarly we might ask ourselves: if the will tends toward the known good all the time, does that mean we never choose evil? If we reflect upon moments of deliberation and choice, it becomes rather clear that this is not the case. It is precisely in deliberation upon and selection of a particular good among many—in relation to our knowledge of who we are and what our potentialities may be—that moral failure occurs. I can freely choose a particular good-for-me-now which I consciously know is not in continuity with my identity and potentialities.[4]

Amid these reflections, however, we must not forget that we also experience our freedom as being severely limited and modified at times. As we have seen, knowledge is of primary importance. We cannot have self-possession if we never arrive at an understanding of the self and its meaning. We cannot choose if we are not aware of options, of different possibilities, of various alternatives. We can neither choose nor love that which we do not in some way know. We

71

might even have experienced people who seemingly never have known goodness, nobility, kindness, or sympathy, and consequently were never able to exercise their freedom with respect to these values. Moreover, there are ample data that point to the importance of environment, conditioning, deprivation, habit, emotion, natural preference, and one's own history in the formation of projects and choices. All of these factors are undeniable, and they must be weighed with the factors that point to man's freedom.

Consequently, reflection upon my experience leads me to conclude at least initially that there are forces which can shape and influence my present and future behavior. Nonetheless, there are also data that cannot be ignored which point to the conclusion that determining "forces" do not totally destroy my ability to take possession of myself. As long as I can question, as long as I can achieve a distance from my environment and from immediate needs, and as long as I can know various values and goods as limited and conditional, I can take hold of my life and my situation and I can say something about it.

In conclusion I might say, first, that I feel free. This is an important consideration. But feeling free does not necessarily make it so. The feeling of freedom does indicate, however, that such an experience is quite primary and fundamental to our behavior. Second and more important is that there are levels of human behavior which, upon reflective analysis, indicate freedom as self-possession and freedom of choice. These levels of behavior, moreover, are not just feelings. They are the incontrovertible evidences of questioning, self-reflection, distance, and the awareness of goods-precisely-as-conditional. If these actions did *not* exist, I could not be doing what I am doing right now.

The Position of Total Determinism

Our previous discussion, however, does not absolve us of the task of investigating a consistent and scholarly deterministic view of man and of reflecting upon its meaning and significance. Many areas might be considered—sociology, genetics, anthropology; but for our purposes here, we will look at a total stimulus-response theory of human behavior. We will not try to imply that all behaviorists are determinists; nor can we even state for sure that B. F. Skinner, the man in particular whom we will treat, is a total philosophical determinist—although he may sound like one.

In his book, *Science and Human Behavior,* Skinner rather clearly states his case: "The hypothesis that man is not free is essential to the application of the scientific method to the study of human behavior. The free inner man who is held responsible for his behavior is only a pre-scientific substitute for the kinds of causes which are discovered in the course of the scientific analysis. All these alternative causes lie outside the individual."[5] Note the following things about this statement. a) Skinner is speaking in the context of the scientific method. In *Walden Two* he points out that the notion of freedom is too sloppy a concept for a man who is interested in prediction and environmental control. As a scientific hypothesis, then, total determinism might be much more fruitful for collecting and interpreting data than the hypothesis of freedom. b) The second point occurs when Skinner extends the position of determinism to the extent that other interpretations of human behavior (e.g., human freedom) are pre-scientific. There seems to be a question as to whether other levels of human explanation—besides the scientific—have any validity. c) Third, Skinner seems to be maintaining that the causes for human action all lie outside the man and that these causes are necessitating. They would *have* to be necessary if my actions are necessarily determined.

Skinner's position seems to be, then, that man's behavior is shaped and determined by external forces and stimuli, whether they be familial or cultural sanction, verbal or non-verbal reinforcement, or complex systems of reward and punishment. I have nothing to say about the course of action which I will take. I apparently cannot question these outside forces which mold my behavior. The implications of this are practically developed in the society of *Walden Two,* where Frazier, apparently Skinner's hero, says, "Well, what do you say to the design of personalities? Would that interest you? The control of temperaments? Give me the specifications and I'll give you the man! What do you say to the control of motivation, building the interests which will make men most productive and most successful? Does that seem to you fantastic? Yet some of the techniques are available and more can be worked out experimentally. Think of the possibilities . . . Let us control the lives of our children and see what we can make of them."[6]

These are not mere claims on Skinner's part. The power of conditioning has been frequently substantiated by research in both human and infra-human levels. Reinforcement can mold a group's reactions. It can turn self-conscious speakers into group leaders. Human reactions and behavior seem to be extremely manipulable. In many cases it appears that individuals can be programmed like a machine whose behavior is not only predicted, but controlled. As a matter of fact, Skinner suggests that this phenomenon is occurring right now in our society—in a rather inefficient way—by means of governmental, educational, and propagandistic control techniques.

When I as a subject reflect upon what Skinner says in *Walden Two* and *Science and Human Behavior,* I see many levels of my own experience which correspond to his position.

a) I have genetic, biological, and physical structures which influence my behavior. They are part of the total me which is involved in choosing.

b) I have environmental structures which are part of me —my early life and psychological development, the culture, national, and ecclesiastical frameworks that I find myself situated in.

c) I am keenly aware of external forces and demands which impinge upon me, sometimes creating needs and even values.

All of these levels of experience mentioned above I can call my historicity; and all of them can be explained by and understood in terms of behavioral control and environmental conditioning. But it is just as evident to me that there are other levels of experience which cannot be explained by or reduced to my historicity.

a) I (and it seems that any being called "man") can make myself aware of my biological and physical limitations, compensating for them, channelling them, improving them.

b) I can question my own environmental structures. I can revolt against them or validate them. I can undergo psychological experiences in order to restructure them. I can challenge them—even as Skinner has challenged them.

c) I can achieve a distance from external demands and forces. I can hesitate, reflect and deliberate, challenge. I can talk about them.

These levels of experience are on the level of free inquiry, or intelligence. They are found in *any* human environment or culture. The level of free inquiry enables me to communicate with other people with quite diverse histories. They enable me to change and challenge my own history. The spheres of historicity and free inquiry cannot be reduced to each other, nor can they be explained away by the other. It seems that absolute determinism attempts to do just that. And it runs into innumerable difficulties.

1. The actions of questioning and self-reflection must be either explained away or ignored. If they are explained away, it would have to be done by using questioning and self-reflection. Ignoring their existence is admitting that one's theory cannot account for them.

2. It cannot be assumed that all causal motives are necessitating causes. Experientially the goods that we confront and the motives that we use are precisely conditional, limited, and mixed.

3. If we are all absolutely determined, then we all must be deluded at the very heart of our primary experience, for it seems that almost all normal men experience some degree of freedom in choosing or being able to say something about their own actions. In fact, it would be difficult to conceive how men could operate at all in this world without at least the "feeling" of being free. Society at

every level—the interpersonal, the legal, the political, the scientific—is based upon the primordial "feeling" or experience of freedom and responsibility. If such a radically basic experience is a delusion, how could we tell whether any basic experience is trustworthy. Philosophy and the scientific enterprise itself could hardly get out of the net of total skepticism and inaction.

4. If all of our judgments and choices are "conditioned" and necessitated by prior reinforcement or external stimuli, this case would have to hold true for the determinist himself. He has not freely responded to the "truth value" of his position; rather he has been forced to accept determinism because of his own past, his own environment, and sanctions that have been put upon him from the outside. It is not a position adhered to because of its logic, feasibility, or coherence. It is a position that he has unwittingly been pushed into. Not only does the total determinist discredit his own position, but he also admits that the very criteria for scientific experimentation which he holds to are merely value judgments which have been assumed because they have been previously accepted by others now in power and who in turn reward or reinforce *him* for accepting them.

These last two problems (3 and 4) with absolute determinism are not actually refutations. They are rather reflections about a totally determined world and the conclusions that flow from it. What is more important, however, is that a total determinist would have a difficult time explaining all levels of human behavior—even his own behavior. If B. F. Skinner is a total determinist (in the philosophical sense), I would like to say about his behavior at least the following things. First, I think that he is more than just a product of "forces" external to him, that he offers his theory not only because it is positively reinforcing. Second, I think that he has not been forced or blindly necessitated to hold his own position. Rather it is only because he has questioned and challenged his past that he is able to offer his theory to other men. Finally, I do not believe that he would communicate at all unless he had an implicit faith in the free questioning intellects of the men to whom he is offering his system. Unless men can freely respond to the value of what he says, the only alternative would be to seize power in order to control their values and mind.[7]

In conclusion, it would seem that determinism as a scientific method has a great deal to offer us in helping us understand how one's historicity influences one's behavior. It is an important level of human explanation. However, as a total explanation of all human behavior, it fails to account for the data of questioning, self-reflection, and intelligent inquiry; and it cannot succeed in validating its own position nor the value of scientific investigation.

If the attempt to reduce man to his historicity and external structures fails, there nonetheless remains the problem of whether man can be reduced to pure structureless freedom without any nature or any history. Consequently, we should make some attempt to understand the position of absolute indeterminism.

The Case for Absolute Freedom

For Jean-Paul Sartre, the fullest realization of one's manhood is found in the recognition that one's very identity is freedom itself. "I *am* my freedom," Orestes shouts to Zeus in *The Flies*.[8] The insight, Orestes says, crashed down upon him out of the blue and swept him off his feet. Zeus performed his greatest blunder when he made man free. Man now became his own king and his own lawgiver.

But as we have seen in the quotation from Sartre at the beginning of this chapter, man is actually free and indeterminate because there is no God to conceive man as a definable essence—God being an absolute metaphysical contradiction. Rather than being an essence, man is the structureless phenomenon of consciousness in the world. Man as consciousness, as a For-itself, is purely a transparent, volatile self-projection continually negating the staticity, structure, and heaviness of the In-itself. And since man in his very identity is an act of negating the In-itself and an act of self-projection, his very meaning and existence is freedom, and his nature is *posterior,* flowing from his own free defining of himself.

Human freedom precedes essence in man and makes it

possible; the essence of the human being is suspended in his freedom. What we call freedom is impossible to distinguish from the *being* of "human reality." Man does not exist *first* in order to be free *subsequently;* there is no difference between the being of man and his *being free.*[9]

Man's freedom is overwhelmingly evident to Sartre because man is able to detach himself from the world by his acts of questioning and doubt. This is so evident, in fact, that the problem of determinism, with its arguments about motivation and causality, is at best tedious. The freewill advocates, he maintains, are killing their efforts in trying to find actions which have no cause. They assume, with the determinists, that a free act must have no cause—a meaningless assumption, having nothing to do with the question of freedom. "Indeed the case could not be otherwise since every action must be *intentional;* each action must, in fact, have an end, and the end in turn is referred to a cause."[10]

> The result is that it is in fact impossible to find an act without a motive but this does not mean that we must conclude that the motive causes the act; the motive is an integral part of the act. For as the resolute project toward a change is not distinct from the act, the motive, the act, and the end are all constituted in a single upsurge. . . . It is the act which decides its ends and its motives, and the act is the expression of freedom.[11]

Certainly, then, there are causes for my actions; but these causes are only part of the total life-project which is me-reaching--outside-of-myself in the act of self-transcending freedom. And since my identity and life-project are indefinable before I actually take a course of action, I am the only source which decides ends, motives, and causes—and I am doing this only when I am exercising my freedom.[12]

Although Sartre seems to maintain that there is always a situation (our historicity and facticity) from which we choose, its influence upon our freedom is inconsequential. Within *any* context, by the very fact that I continually overreach myself in choices and formation of projects—as my very identity—there is only the future which I set up for myself. The past has no effect upon my choices because there is no deliberation in making them. I do not choose in the light of past choices and reflection upon them. By the very fact that I am conscious, I choose.[13]

The position of Sartre, consequently, is diametrically opposed to that of Skinner.

a) Since man's very identity as a For-itself involves consciousness and freedom as immediate givens, and since both involve negation of the structures of the In-itself (definition, staticity, heaviness) man is not tied down by his facticity and the world in which he finds himself. Rather his existence is resistance-to and transcendence-from them, because he can negate them. Freedom's very meaning is a struggle with and a negation of what is *given*.

b) Since freedom is involved with the future and freedom is man's identity, man is not tied down by his past or by the choices of the past. Thus one's history, one's environment, and one's past motivation in no way hinder his freedom.

c) There is no definable limitation to my identity, since I choose my own identity and I make my own essence. Freedom and structure are reciprocally contradictory.

As opposed to Skinner's total emphasis upon the past, upon one's historicity, and upon one's environment, Sartre places total emphasis on the future, the ability to question and revolt, the phenomenon of distance and transcendence. Oddly enough, many of our own initial concepts of freedom tend to one or other of these polarities. We can be overwhelmed by the notion of determinism and historicity—as we have seen in our discussion of Skinner; and we can be equally captivated by the opposite solution of total freedom.

Any notion of freedom which denies the importance of structure is similar to that of Sartre. Moreover, when one affirms that freedom is opposed to structure, one will eventually have to choose between absolute freedom (structurelessness) or absolute determinism (total structure). I myself will fall into this dilemma if I think that freedom involves a negation of external imposition, of binding commitments, of my past, and an affirmation of pure, spontaneous, unreflective, and unencumbered action.

Sartre is certainly incisive in his analysis of man's ability to question, to negate, and to form a life-project. But how can he account for the data that Skinner presents about man's historicity, and how can he deal with the facts of our own experience which indicate that external and internal structures enter into our choices?

The facts of experimental psychology, biology, and sociology stand strongly in the face of the conjecture that we might be totally free of external influence, hereditary factors, environmental tugs, and normal psychophysical development. I am inextricably bound to who I am, and "who I am" includes my history, my growth, and the total formation of the life which I have led to this moment—*as well as* my ability to question, to negate, and to achieve a distance from necessity. To be *me* involves the structure of *what* being me is; and wherever I may go or flee, I will carry myself with me. Whether I have parents in the Communist Party or whether I have been a member of the resistance with a pious bourgeois family (as is the case with Sartre), or whether I have dropped out from a middle-class-split-level-suburban-society, I cannot annihilate my past, my identity, nor my potentialities. And having a past, a history, and an identity as a self-transcending animal, I of necessity embrace the very structure of my identity, my drives, and my meaning. I cannot hide from the rules of my physical being or my historicity, nor can I escape the structure of my demand to know, love, and possess myself. If I am to be related to anyone, I must take on structure; if I am to make any project for myself, I must take on a structure; if I am, like Sartre, to forswear "bad faith," I am taking on structure in that very commitment. To deny structure is to assume one. The very concept of fidelity itself entails structure. If to be without structure is to be free, it is a strange type of freedom. It is like the freedom of a rock—feeling no misery, no pain, as the song goes—hardly a claim to grandeur.

Structured Freedom: Human Reality

Sartre and Skinner, as we have seen, concentrate on levels of human reality to the exclusion of other levels. One realm covers man's historicity and given structures; the other realm covers man's transcendence in free questioning. Skinner focuses on the first. Consequently he stresses man's physical, genetic, biological facticity, the external structures of environmental, psychological, and historical "givens," and the way in which man's present has been conditioned by the history of his past. Sartre, on the other hand, concentrates on the second. Thus he emphasizes man's release from immediate, blind demands and his ability to shape and confront his facticity. In addition, he dwells on man's ability to question, to negate or validate external "givens," and on his openness to knowledge and love. But the point is that integral human existence includes both of these realms or levels. Consequently, if man is free, his freedom will involve both realms of his experience, and any interpretation of man must be able to integrate both realms. Absolute determinism either omits the data of transcendence and questioning or tries to reduce it to external "forces." Absolute indeterminism ignores man's history and structure or tries to wish it out of existence.

The problem is that neither area can be reduced to the other, and yet both exist quite obviously in our experience. As Maslow said (in the citation given at the beginning of this chapter), environment is important in the development of my potentialities as a man, but environment does not give them to me. He agrees with Sartre in that man can form his own life project, and yet he nods to Skinner in admitting the importance of the environment in helping these potentialities become actualized.

Our own experience and the experience of other men testify to the mutual importance of both realms. When I am most fully functioning, I find that my own self possession is not at odds with the structures in my life. Actually I find that freedom and structure are complementaries rather than contradictories. The free man does not necessarily fight structure. Internal structures of his very manhood emerge with his maturation. In the process of his growth he either internalizes external structures or rejects them as inauthentic with respect to his manhood. Much like an animal we suffer a growing process in which demands, needs, and responses are largely determined by the external world in which we find ourselves immersed. But with the emergence of questioning (due to the given structure of being-a-human) and the philosophical freedom it entails, we are able to confront the externals of environment, country, history, and evaluate them, reject them, or validate them by making them our own.

Even if a man were to try to reject all structure, he would in the very act of rejection tie himself to the structure of rejection; the self, in order to be a self, must have some structure to operate at all. At least the self, willy-nilly, has the structure of being a self with various demands and potentialities. And since we are questioning selves, structure will flow from our actual identity—the structure of the demands and drives to know and to do something about what we know. The fact of being human will give rise to structures, values, and demands which will not militate against my freedom, but which will actually make freedom possible and enhance it. As Carl Rogers has said, "Instead of universal values 'out there' or a universal value system imposed by some group—philosophers, priests, or psychologists—we have the possibility of universal human value directions emerging from the experiencing of the human organism."[14]

Often the values which "emerge" from one's own humanness will be quite close to the values and structured systems "imposed" by the status quo of other human beings who are already here before us. These are the values and structures which we will freely internalize. Often again, these emergent values will be opposed to the present order, especially if the present order has been unfaithful to its potentialities and identity. These "surpressed" potentialities will, as Maslow says, "clamor to be realized." In this case, freedom and free philosophical questioning become the prosecutors of the present and the prophets of the future. This is perhaps what the history of philosophy is all about—the criticism of human failure and the affirmation of forgotten human possibilities.

Structure, then, is not only compatible with freedom; it is fundamental to all human growth, evolution, and process. Freedom is exercised only within the structure of one's humanity and one's historicity; and it is the vehicle by which one can remain faithful to one's humanity and history. In conclusion we might say:

a) Structures are the offerings of the human world to which I come. Structures embrace historicity, environment, the community of thought, cultural and moral heritage.

b) Structure is also the internal constitution of being a man with human potentialities. It is the reason why values and demands emerge from my own identity as a questioning self, a knower, a lover.

c) My own freely created life project is also a structure. The structure of being a man is the basis of internally *self-constituted* values which I share with the world of other selves who have the same internal dynamisms.

Freedom is operative on all levels, if I want to make it so; and it is operative not as a force against structure, but as a force *emerging from* structure and *merging with* structure in order to further actualize individual and species-wide human potentialities. Man is neither absolutely free nor absolutely determined. Man is freedom within structure.

A Note on Freedom and Anxiety

The controversy between freedom and determinism sometimes seems to pale before the problem of whether freedom is a good thing to have in the first place. For many, the problem is not in proving the freedom of the will; rather it is in accepting its true meaning and consequences. More explicitly, freedom can be a lonely and terrifying thing.

83

> Freedom is not a reward or a decoration that is celebrated with champagne . . . Oh, no! It's a chore, on the contrary, and a long distance race, quite solitary and very exhausting. No champagne, no friends raising their glasses as they look to you affectionately. Alone in a forbidden room, alone in the prisoner's box, before judges, and alone to decide in the face of oneself or in the face of others' judgment. At the end of all freedom is a court sentence; that's why freedom is too heavy to bear, especially when you're down with a fever, or distressed, or love nobody.[15]

Unlike Camus writing *The Fall,* many of us try to conceive freedom as if it were something like the effortless flight of a bird. Unfortunately, it often turns out not to be the easy thing that we might have expected. Since it is part of our very identity, when freedom starts to hurt, we often try to shed it like an extra hat—or at least forget about it. When this fails, the only thing left for us to do is to try to change it into something other than it is—a decoration, a badge, a formula. But it is no decoration, and there are no hurrahs from cheering crowds. There are no toasts to it. There is no escape from it. As Sartre says, in a way we are condemned to be free.

Moreover, in the exercise of freedom, we are definitively and ultimately alone. Only we can possess ourselves. No one else can do it for us. And most terrifying of all, our choices are irrevocable, since the present moment is never to be repeated. We cannot redo what we have chosen. We can only summon ourselves to manage making a new choice. I must be my own man; this is said to be my glory. No one can take my place or receive my blame; this is my suffering as a man. I must freely create a life-project which is myself, extending myself into further realms of existence. And I alone am accountable.

> As soon as we lend our minds to the essence of human responsibility, we cannot forbear to shudder; there is something fearful about man's responsibility. But at the same time something glorious! Every moment holds thousands of possibilities but we can choose only a single one of

these; all the others we have condemned, damned to non-being—and that too, for all eternity. But it is glorious to know that the future of the things and the people around us, is dependent—even if only to a tiny extent—upon our decision at any given moment. What we actualize by that decision, what we thereby bring into the world, is saved; we have conferred reality upon it and preserved it from passing.[16]

Viktor Frankl places the problem well in this passage. Freedom, which is the basis of man's dignity and glory, which is the synthesis of his knowing and loving powers, is also the source of human ambiguity. Hence, it is terrible and it is beautiful. Sartre is quite honest, then, not only in placing freedom on such a high pedestal, but also in seeing it as something of a condemnation and judgment.

I can create the project that is myself and seek out all the possible horizons of my potentialities. And I can ruin myself. In my free choices, I damn the alternatives to non-being, and I bring into existence a creative action, which—but for me—would never have been brought into existence. Hence freedom is not at all an easy thing; rather, it is a two-edged sword of ambiguous possibilities.

The major ambiguity about human freedom is that man is able to know that he is free, what his identity is, what his potentialities are, and he is able to say something about it. Here, we should remember what we discovered about the nature of man's identity as a knower and a wanter. Radically, knowledge and love have internal dynamisms which are outward and self-transcending rather than appropriative and grasping. By my very identity as a questioner I am thrust out of my encapsulated self. I am carried into the world of the other, into the entire cosmos. Very simply, they are open rather than closed dynamisms.

What is most important, however, is that human knowledge and love are open by nature, but not by necessity. Openness is a difficult, delicate thing—as we have seen and will see—and I can choose to remain closed. I can opt for being the center and horizon of my own world, to collect rather than to break out. And here is the rub: I can freely, irrevocably choose to be closed, to be an event which is in its very dynamism open, but which—in freedom—has opted for self-enclosure.

Here again, we can understand why man would at times want to avoid the terror of the choice, why he would sometimes opt to be secure and tensionless in a necessitated nature, rather than insecure and anxious in the freedom of making himself. We can see why he might not want to choose at all, rather than face the task of self-condemnation, why he might try to hand over his freedom either by ignorance or by wanting someone else to choose for him. Dostoevsky sees this when his Grand Inquisitor in *The Brothers Karamazov* indicts Christ for bringing man the terrible gift of freedom which has caused man such suffering.[17] But the Inquisitor, in saving man from choice, has reduced man to the status of a flock of sheep, contented with food, authority, and force.

This is the greatest problem with freedom: it is terrible, but if you take it away, you take away my meaning, my dignity, and my creativity. Such is the case as it is posed in Huxley's *Brave New World,* when John, the savage, challenges the Controller by saying, "But I don't want comfort. I want God, I want poetry, I want real danger, I want freedom, I want goodness, I want to sin."[18] Human dignity and human ambiguity are of the same cloth. If you take away the ambiguities of life, if you take away the tensions, if you take away the difficulties of choice and the suffering of doubt, you take away my freedom, emasculating me and preventing me from significantly creative action. Freedom and guilt, anxiety, tension, responsibility are not mutually exclusive; in the human condition they help comprise the total meaning of man.

But all is not bleak with freedom. It is also the basis of the most important and fulfilling action a man can place. A man can know himself. Consequently he can possess himself and his destiny. However his destiny and meaning is other-directed, open in his potentialities to know and love. As a result, man's meaning is not only to possess himself freely. Since he is other-directed, his identity is not fully achieved until, having possessed himself, he gives himself to the other.

FREEDOM OF CONSCIOUSNESS
John Wild[19]

We say that an act is indeterminate if it might have been otherwise. But if we ignore the awareness dwelling in every human act, and place this act within an objective, causal frame, such a statement fails to fit the frame, and seems to be impossible. We all know the way in which recent analysts have argued that it can mean: this act might have been otherwise *if the situation had been different*. With the *if* clause, freedom here vanishes into a normal, objective, causal sequence. Those of us who have studied the long history of this controversy also know the way similar moves have been used in the past by determinists who, in my opinion, have had, on the whole, by far the better of such arguments. When restricted to an isolated act of will, which is placed in an objective perspective of this sort, freedom has little chance.

But perhaps freedom is something far more basic. Perhaps it cannot be restricted to a specific kind of act which can be regarded objectively in this way. Perhaps, as Kant realized, it belongs in a world of its own, the *Lebenswelt* of our daily life, which lies beyond the objective perspectives of science and of objective thought in general, and which Kant, therefore, still a rationalist in this respect, mistakenly regarded as *noumenal*. Perhaps it cannot be properly understood as any object or set of objects *in* the *Lebenswelt* but rather as a necessary phase of this world-consciousness itself. Let us try to make these statements plausible by suggesting a contrast with which we are all in some degrees familiar.

There is a mode of immediate experience, as we sometimes call it, in which we gain no distance from the so-called object. We pay no attention to *what it is*. Our whole attention is directed rather to changing it, and mastering it for the satisfaction of some desire. We have little self-awareness. As we sometimes say, we are lost in our pursuit. At the same time, our field of awareness narrows to the immediate situation determined by our need. We lose our sense of the world as a whole, of the past as well as the future. Our immediate experience here and now simply carries us along.

This, of course, describes an ideal limit which can only be approximated by men. It is a reasonable guess, however, that it applies fairly accurately to the experience of animals where language, in the strict sense of this term, is lacking. Such experience is pragmatically determined. Hence we do not call it *free*. We say of persons in such a condition that they are obsessed and have lost their sense of reality. When we talk to them, we feel that they are not wholly present to themselves (not themselves) and not wholly present to us. Let us now contract this condition with the more authentic order of awareness from which it is, in man, a deviation.

This mode of awareness is not content merely to follow the immediate flux of pragmatically determined experience. It has accepted another standard, the standard of reality, to judge its thoughts and actions. I am not content with the given date. I become aware of *things* confronting me, and I want to know *what they really are*. I am present to myself, and I wish to know and to become what I really am, not merely on the background of my familiar needs and attitudes, but on the background of a broader horizon which encompasses all that is, and to which we refer sometimes as *being* and sometimes as *the world*. Let us now ask ourselves what lies at the root of these distinctive traits of human consciousness.

I believe that if we raise this question seriously, we shall find that this is a self-negation or self-transcendence, only one partial aspect of which has been inadequately expressed by the notion of indeterminism. Man is the being who can say *no* not only to others but to himself. This is the root from which our freedom and responsibility grow. Let us see if we can clarify this by a few brief indications.

First of all, if my awareness is to free itself from the biological determinism of animal experience, it must be able to achieve a distance from what is given, to get away from the drives that glue it to this given, and to confront it as a real thing in the world. This is a basic fact of our human awareness, which is ecstatic or outside itself, always giving itself up to what is other than itself. But in order to do this, it must first gain a distance from itself that is missing in the animal. It can identify itself with what we call *an object* only from this distance. Our awareness actively confronts the beings it knows. It irrupts into them and makes them present as real things, or to use the ancient analogy, it brings them out of the darkness into the light.

But in order to become other and to identify with them in this way, our consciousness must first free itself from what it is already. Only by gaining this distance from the given, can it win that openness to what is other than itself, which is the heart and core of what we mean by freedom. This being-open-to-otherness (freedom) is found in every basic manifestation of human consciousness. Thus the animal can understand a sign which is manifestly related to its "signatum." But it cannot take an arbitrary element of its experience as a way of regarding something else that is absent. Hence language in the strict sense is beyond its capacity. Our imagination enables us to take any given experience as related to something with which it is not related, and to see it as what it is *not*.

The question *why* lies at the root of our efforts to gain intellectual understanding. *Why,* we ask, is it this way and not some other? It is only by first separating ourselves from our original experience that things may be revealed as they *are,* in their being, and brought into the light. It is only by first becoming absent from him that I can truly become present to another.

The same holds true of my presence to myself. As our language indicates, this is a self-relatedness based on a prior self-separation, of which the animal is incapable. It simply is what it is. Man, on the other hand, is never just what he is but always other, so that he can be present to himself, thinking with himself as *con-scious* or as *con-science.* This primordial, *thinking with,* does not originally mean staring at myself in an objective perspective. This is a special and later derivation. Originally it means a lived awareness of my whole being-in-the-world of which I am the center, for I am not an isolated thing at an instant, here and now.

I *am* my lived body. But I am also outside this body *in* the various regions of my concern—in the book that I am reading, in the work that I am doing, in its tools and in its objects. I am also the past that I have been, and the projects I have projected into my future ahead of me. Of all this, during my waking moments and in certain ways even during sleep, I am dimly aware in a pre-thematic way, within the broad horizon of my life-world, the *Lebenswelt*. All these things, past and present, and I myself, are in this world-horizon that belongs essentially to my lived awareness. What can we say of this horizon as against other backgrounds, such as what is not called the *life-field* of an animal?

It is interesting to note that this biological concept of the life-field is similar to that of the human life-world, and that they were both worked out at approximately the same time. The discoveries of J. von Uexkull, the German biologist, and his school from 1920 to 1930 were particularly important in breaking down the traditional conception of a single material environment which remains the same for all species and all individual organisms. Von Uexkull showed that this is an abstract construction which has no real importance in understanding the life of a given species. What is important here is the life-field *(Umwelt)* into which the animal's action radiates, and where it can be present. The nature of this life-field is correlated with the projects of the animal and grounded on the peculiar anatomy of each species, which thus has an environment of its own. Each individual member of the species lives in its own field, and is sensitive to any invasion of this field by alien forces. Such invasions will lead to a life-and-death struggle.

In this country, George H. Mead developed similar conceptions of the mutual interdependence of the living animal and its environment. No living organism can be adequately understood without an understanding of its life-field. The inner cycles of its bodily life define an objective territory with certain traits which are necessary to its existence. This existence depends on the field which conditions it. But the field depends on the type of organism which carves it out and gives it vital meaning. This is a strange *sui generis* relationship in which each factor is conditioned by the other, and which cannot be understood in terms of cause and effect. To live is to radiate. Hence each individual plant and animal not only has, but must have, a vital field into which its existence is projected.

The human being is no exception to this rule. He also has his vital field or habitat, where he knows his way and where his presence is radiated. He has the house and the family where he is at home; the carpenter has his shop where he works; the scholar his library where he studies and the classroom where he argues and teaches; the farmer his field and barns where he lives on the land. The individual becomes attached to his vital field and cannot be separated from it without becoming displaced and disoriented, as the city man in the country or the peasant who gropes for his way in the city. Without roots in a vital field of this kind, the normal person can do nothing.

But this human world differs from the animal field in the two vital respects we have suggested. In the first place, unlike the animal, man can get at a distance from his field, reveal it as it is, and thus become open to a being other than his own. The radical freedom of awareness has enabled different *cultures,* as we call them, to order different meaningful horizons, and different individuals, even in the same culture, to work out radically different styles of life and different horizons of their own. There is a freedom of world-formation, closely connected with what we call philosophy. This is the first difference.

But the second is equally important. Our awareness is free. It can negate itself, and out of this nothingness reveal the being of what confronts it as it is. But this freedom is finite. It is limited by the situation into which it has been thrown and by the special projects to which it has access. It cannot escape from history, which, at any given time, makes certain things more accessible and conceals others.

What is revealed is understood in perspective, always ambiguous in certain respects. Hence while we shed some light around us, this light fades into shadow. The truth we reveal is always partial and necessarily mixed with error. Though this has sometimes been denied by dogmatic philosophers, it is known to the pre-thematic and primordial understanding of men. Hence, though I may be living in a world of my own quite different from that of Jones, we are both able to make an important distinction between *my* world, or *my version of the world,* and what we call *the world* as it really is, which includes all that we see truly as we see it, our false seeing, and much more. It is this openness to the radical otherness of transcendence, as we may call it, which makes communication between different styles of life, and even different schools of philosophy, always possible. In fact, this possibility of communication between radically divergent worlds and styles of life is one of the most important disciplines to be learned from the study of philosophy, the discipline which pushes our awareness to its farthest limits and even beyond, and, is therefore, in a peculiarly appropriate sense the discipline of freedom for it is our human awareness that is, as such, self-transcendent and free.

This, of course, is only a brief sketch . . . . If, as I believe, it is on the whole sound, freedom is not a mere derivative trait founded on reason. Rather, that which is most essentially human about our consciousness, including what we call "reason," is founded on freedom. In order to understand anything, not merely as it fits our needs, but *as it really is,* we must negate our ever-present pragmatic attitudes to win distance from it. This requires intensive discipline and struggle. Only by emptying ourselves in this way can we achieve that openness to other being, that ability to conceive things otherwise, sometimes called imagination, which is the source of freedom.

It is only through the exercise of this conscious negativity that we can transcend the utilitarianism which rules the animal kingdom and a great part of our human life. Out of this nothingness, being can be revealed, and we can gain some access not merely to things as they are in *my* world for me, but to things as they are in *the world.* Then instead of using them or mastering them, we may have the courage to respect them and to *let them be* as they are.

1. B.F. Skinner, *Walden Two,* (New York: Macmillan, 1962, paperback), p. 258. Hardback edition published in 1948.

2. Jean-Paul Sartre, "Existentialism is a Humanism," from Walter Kaufmann, *Existentialism from Dostoevsky to Sartre* (New York: Meridian Books, 1956), pp. 290-291. The lecture of Sartre's, translated by Mairet, has also been published in a small hardbound edition.

3. Abraham Maslow, *Toward a Psychology of Being* (Princeton: Insight Van Nostrand, 1962), pp. 151-152.

4. Some philosophers have questioned how the intellect and the will work together in the act of free choice. By my intellect, I know what I know—and I am not "free" in this respect. Inasmuch as I know various options, various goods are presented to the will by the intellect. The intellect here is operating as a basis for the will's final causality. Since these eligible goods are not seen as unconditional goods, the will is not necessitated to any particular good and can determine the intellect to what is called the "last practical judgment," the will doing this by efficient causality. As Royce points out in his text, "The will directs the intellect, so to speak, to focus upon this aspect of goodness." This seems to be a reasonable explanation of the causality involved.

5. B. F. Skinner, *Science and Human Behavior* (New York: Macmillan, 1953), p. 447. This citation, as well as my own previous comments, should be balanced by Skinner's contention that man can in ways modify his future environment. The point remains difficult to see, however, if the "self" is adequately defined as a "functionally unified system of *responses*" (page 285; my emphasis). The critical issue often seems to be whether there is indeed a real—in some ways autonomous and initiating—self.

6. B. F. Skinner, *Walden Two,* p. 292.

7. Many other criticisms have been offered. Two of them, centered around the notion of scientific objectivity, maintain that all knowledge is committed knowledge (even scientific criteria are based

on value judgments) and that the neat cause-effect universe of the behaviorist is based upon an outdated Cartesian and Newtonian view of knowledge and scientific investigation. See Carl R. Rogers, "Freedom and Commitment," a reprint from Western Behavioral Institute, pp. 14-15. The entire article, in fact, is helpful. See also the books by May, Maslow, and Matson listed in the following bibliography.

8. Jean-Paul Sartre, *No Exit and Three Other Plays* (New York: Vintage Books, 1946), p. 121. The entire play is about the problem of freedom and man's relation to God.

9. Jean-Paul Sartre, *Being and Nothingness,* Translated with an Introduction by Hazel Barnes. (New York: Citadel Press, Second Paperback Edition, 1965), p. 25. All emphases are in this text.

10. *Ibid.,* p. 412.

11. *Ibid.,* pp. 413-414.

12. *Ibid.,* pp. 412-418 passim. The entire section would have to be quoted to give justice to the development of his thought. Any oversimplification, it seems, surely tends to distort his total position.

13. "We must insist on the fact that the question here is not of a deliberate choice. This is not because the choice is *less* conscious or *less* explicit than a deliberation, but rather because it is the foundation of all deliberation and because as we have seen, a deliberation requires an interpretation in terms of an original choice . . . One must be conscious in order to choose, and one must choose in order to be conscious. Choice and consciousness are one and the same thing." *Ibid.,* pp. 437-438.

14. Carl Rogers, "Toward a Modern Approach to Values," from *The Journal of Abnormal and Social Psychology,* Vol. 68, No. 2, 1964, p. 167. Most of Rogers' essays and lectures can be ordered from the Western Behavioral Institute, 1121 Torrey Pines Road, La Jolla, California, 92037.

15. Albert Camus, *The Fall* (New York: Vintage, 1956), pp. 132-133.

16. Viktor Frankl, *The Doctor and the Soul* (New York: Bantam, 1967), p. 28. There is also a hard-bound edition available from libraries.

17. Fyodor Dostoevsky, *Brothers Karamazov.* Special Edition

of the Grand Inquisitor. Introduction by Anne Fremantle. (New York: Unger Publishing Company, 1956) pp. 1-21.

18. Aldous Huxley, *Brave New World* (New York: Bantam Books, 1958), p. 163.

19. John Wild, *Existence and the World of Freedom* (Englewood Cliffs: Prentice-Hall, Inc., 1963), pp. 108-113. Reprinted by permission of Prentice-Hall, Inc., Englewood Cliffs, New Jersey.

It should be noted for any bibliography, and especially for one that follows a chapter concerned with the problem of freedom, that the selectivity involved is necessarily judgmental and even perhaps prejudicial. Just as the existentialists are only one wing of contemporary philosophy (itself being a fragment on the entire spectrum of philosophical thought), so also the reference to the psychologists listed below—with the exception of Skinner—is severely limited in scope. Those listed, however, in some way point out a few of the aspects treated in the present chapter.

Camus, Albert. *The Fall*. New York: Vintage, 1956. All of Camus' work is challenging, well written and profound. See also the novel, *The Plague. The Myth of Sisyphus* is a short essay dealing with problem of suicide in the face of man's confrontation with absurdity and limit-situations.

Frankl, Viktor. *Man's Search for Meaning*. New York: Washington Square Press, 1963. Originally titled, "From Death Camp to Existentialism," it is a unique testimony to the possibilities of environment-transcendence.

———. *The Doctor and the Soul*. New York: Bantam, 1967. A deeper and more extensive presentation of Frankl's theories, this book has some striking insights into the nature of attitudinal freedom and the nature of responsibility.

Fromm, Erich. *Man For Himself*. Greenwich: Fawcett Premier, 1965. This book incorporates most of *The Art of Loving* and is an attempt to set up a natural-law system of ethics. See also *Escape from Freedom* and the last chapter of *The Heart of Man* (devoted to a mediated resolution for the problem of determinism).

Hook, Sidney (ed.). *Determinism and Freedom.* New York: Collier, 1961. A series of readings and statements by scientists and philosophers on the notion of freedom. For the most part, the selections make different approaches to the problem than we have been considering—frequently centering on the nature of causality rather than phenomenological analyses of the free act.

Huxley, Aldous. *Brave New World.* New York: Bantam, 1932. This, along with Orwell's *1984*, is an interesting and unsympathetic treatment of the fixed environment and closed society. Huxley makes a brilliant case for freedom, non-probative as it may be at the end of the last chapter.

Malcolm X. *Autobiography of Malcolm X.* New York: Grove Press, 1966. This book, like Claude Brown's *Manchild in a Promised Land,* is worth reading for countless reasons, one of which is to see and to some extent experience the dialectic of the free human act emerging from and transcending the environment.

Marcel, Gabriel. *The Philosophy of Existentialism.* New York: Citadel, 1956. The incisive second chapter offers a possible alternative to Sartre's notion of human existence and freedom.

Matson, Floyd. *The Broken Image.* Garden City, N.Y.: Doubleday Anchor Books, 1966. A stimulating treatment of the sciences and their relation to man's alienation. It is a strong appeal for many levels of human explanation, not just the positivistic or reductionistic. A similar appeal, with a quite different methodology, is offered by Arthur Koestler in his *Ghost in the Machine,* a much more polemic statement.

May, Rollo. *Psychology and the Human Dilemma.* Princeton: Van Nostrand, 1966. Deals with the problem of alienation and anxiety. Two of the chapters are explicitly directed against behavioristic determinism.

Murray, John C. (ed.). *Freedom and Man*. New York: Kenedy, 1965. The series of essays in this book deals with the problems of faith and its relation to freedom.

Rogers, Carl. Reprints from Western Behavioral Sciences Institute. "Freedom and Commitment," as an appealing answer to Skinner. "The Concept of the Fully Functioning Person," "Learning to Be Free," a thoughtful and incisive alternative to determinism.

Royce, Joseph. *The Encapsulated Man*. Princeton: Van Nostrand, 1965. An appeal for the "generalist" multi-leveled approach to man as an open, non-reductive subject of study.

Sartre, Jean-Paul. *Being and Nothingness,* tr. by Hazel Barnes. New York: Washington Square Press, 1966. This edition is cheaper in cost and yet more valuable than the Citadel (abridged) edition whose pagination is used in this chapter. Part Four is particularly concerned with freedom, although it would be somewhat difficult understanding it without having read Parts One and Two.

———. *No Exit and Three Other Plays*. New York: Vintage, 1946. Includes Orestes' self-liberation in *The Flies*. *No Exit* is a compelling literary presentation of Sartre's theory of inter-subjectivity (at least prior to 1950).

Skinner, B. F. *Science and Human Behavior*. New York: Macmillan, 1953. Now in paperback under Free Press, this is a powerful book, challenging one's notions on almost every level of investigation in the philosophy of man.

———. *Walden Two*. New York: Macmillan, 1948. A novelform adventure in an appealingly deterministic utopia. Could be read in conjunction with other utopias, since it gives an unusually affirmative judgment. There has been much reaction to both of these books not only by fellow psychologists, but by literary men and journalists. Some have been insightful, many intemperate at times. Cf. Joseph Wood Krutch's *The Measure of Man.*

Wild, John. *Existence and the World of Freedom.* Englewood, New Jersey: Prentice Hall, 1965. This book has struck me as the most thought-provoking book I have read by a contemporary philosopher, not only for its synthesis of many mind-frames, but for the possibilities it opens up to one who is seriously beginning to philosophize.

Chapter Five

The Drive To Give Oneself Away

"There's no need for red-hot pokers. Hell is —other people!"[1]

Garcin, in Jean-Paul Sartre's *No Exit.*

The truth--that love is the ultimate and the highest goal to which man can aspire. Then I grasped the meaning of the greatest secret that human poetry and human thought and belief have to impart: The salvation of man is through love and in love.[2]

Viktor Frankl

It often seems that there are only two basic views that one might take toward life in general and toward human life in particular. One could reflect upon wars, crime, exploitation, or economics, and perhaps even biology, and conclude that all forms of life are fundamentally grasping and appropriative. In particular, human life and endeavors might seem to be a continual striving to overcome, assimilate, and consume the other. Sometimes, the following words seem pre-eminently true concerning the relations between men: "While I attempt to free myself from the hold of the Other, the Other is trying to free himself from the hold of mine; while I seek to enslave the Other, the Other seeks to enslave me."[3]

On the other hand, we continually run upon evidence that points to an opposite conclusion about life and human relationships. Life might seem to be a process of unfolding and opening-up. People and nations not only struggle; they also promote the growth and fulfillment of others. Sacrificial gifts of individual creativity constantly emerge from artistic minds. People achieve their greatest 'self-actualization, not in conflict, but in mutual encouragement and aspiration.

What is to be made of this? Are these two fundamental oppositions so contradictory that man must be reduced to one or the other? If there are data in our life that testify to the validity of both concepts, can we honestly as reflective beings fail to integrate both of them in our total view of man? If we investigate what we have discovered so far about man's potentialities, we might find a resolution which integrates both viewpoints.

Man, like any other finite nature, has an internal dynamism as a unified organism toward its fullest actualization. As we have seen, we find ourselves in a condition which drives us to question our identity and purpose so that we might somehow validate our existence. In the pursuit of the answer of our identity, we found out that as questioners, knowers, and wanters, our basic identity involves an openness and direction to the other. Consequently, it seems that our identity as men—our nature—involves the unique situation that self-fulfillment and actualization occur *only* when the self is directed outward from itself to the world of things and persons. Our potentialities are fulfilled, then, not by collecting and adding things to ourselves; rather they are fulfilled by being faithful to their basic outward dynamisms. Every organism has the primary need to fulfill its finality and purpose. Nevertheless, the "need" in man takes on the strange characteristic of a love which is not "needing" but rather giving.

Knowing thrusts me, in an act of intentionality, out toward the other—not that I might appropriate it or have power over it, but that I might be invaded by its presence and brought out of my own encapsulation. The tendency which follows upon this type of knowing is not one of grasping, but one of wanting the "other" to be just the way it is because it is good. I do not want to make the other part of me. I would rather become part of it, not by changing it, but by being *with* it and *in* it.

Such a union cannot be enforced by either of the subjects. The

101

only way the union can take place is by the free gift of the self to the other. Thus at the foundation of any loving relationship will be the attitude of gift. The other cannot buy me or collect me; I must freely accept the invitation in an act of giving myself. And, of course, since I cannot give what I do not have, I must be in possession of myself. I must be free. The only thing that one cannot take by force is the love of the other. This is the great thing about human love. It is a gift. And it is actually the only thing that any human being can give—that is, the only thing that any person can fully possess, his own self.

It seems in conclusion, then, that man does operate out of need and the desire for self-fulfillment. With man, however, self-fulfillment is achieved only in self-divestment. Man's greatest *need* is not to operate out of need, but rather to operate because of his drive to *give*. Thus, the dilemma about egocentrism and altruism which we mentioned at the beginning seems to have a possible solution. Just as every other organism, man has an internal drive to fulfill himself and achieve self-actualization. However in the case of the total human organism, self-fulfillment entails a radical openness to the *other*, because of the basic outward drives of the intellect and will. The major problem is, that in our awareness of contingency and "need" for some type of self-validation, the most immediate solution often appears to be in terms of appropriation and power. Self-fulfillment is achieved, not in isolation, but in union. As Erich Fromm has said:

> In contrast to symbiotic union, mature *love* is a *union under the condition of preserving one's integrity,* one's individuality. *Love is an active power in man;* a power which breaks through the walls which separate man from his fellow men, which unites him with others; love makes him overcome the sense of isolation and separateness, yet it permits him to be himself, to retain his integrity. In love the paradox occurs that two beings become one and yet remain two.[4]

Self-actualization and love of the other are not opposites. Rather they are mutually related necessities for human fulfillment.

The Human Potentialities of Sexual Love

In treating the potentialities for human sexual love, it might be best to reflect upon the observations of other men and consider whether their observations correspond at all to our own experience.

The first man we will consider is Viktor Frankl, who—having lived through the ultimately challenging experiences of a concentration-camp prisoner—is overwhelmingly impressed by the power and potentialities of human love.

> In Love the beloved is comprehended in his very essence, as the unique and singular being that he is; he is comprehended as a Thou, and as such is taken into the self. As a person he becomes for the one who loves him indispensable and irreplaceable without having done anything to bring this about. The person who is loved "can't help" having the uniqueness and singularity of his self—that is, the value of his personality—realized. Love is not deserved, is unmerited—it is simply grace.[5]

I see the other person, not as an instrument or a tool to be used, but as another unique creative project, never to be reduplicated nor to be reduced to anyone else. The other person has value, even of himself, without respect to me and the value that I might ascribe to him. The other presents himself as an "invitation" for me to respond to the beauty of personhood which resides there in him. And when I respond to that invitation, the horizons of my possibilities as a man are enlarged.

> But love is not only grace; it is also enchantment. For the lover it casts a spell upon the world, envelops the world in added worth. Love enormously increases receptivity to the fullness of values. The gates to the whole universe of values

103

are, as it were, thrown open. Thus, in his surrender to the Thou the lover experiences an inner enrichment which goes beyond that Thou; for him the whole cosmos broadens and deepens in worth, glows in the radiance of these values which only the lover sees. For it is well known that love does not only make one blind but seeing—able to see values.[6]

If I reflect upon this in my own life, I might see that such a phenomenon occurs. I might ask myself why I love some person, and—outside of her uniqueness—come to the awareness that it was her warmth, her sensitivity, her tenderness, her goodness, her beauty, her sincerity, her openness to me. At first these values might seem so real in her that I might think that she is the actual summation of them. But she knows—and I will consequently know—that she was the limited and imperfect incarnation of values that I had never before really seen or responded to.

When a lover opens himself to another person, he is opening himself to the world of all the values that he sees in the beloved but cannot be reduced to her. She will be the first to claim so—to such an extent that she is responding to these very values precisely because of his love for her. In loving, then, he not only expands his own capacity to respond to the universe around him; what is even more amazing is that the beloved, well knowing that she is not the source of all that he ascribes to her, that she does not exhaust the values which the lover sees in her, wants to grow in those values to which he responds and sees in her. This is the creative side of human love in which two persons are enhanced by the free response of the other, and thereby give birth to broader and deeper values. In other words, a person who is loved changes just as much as the one who loves him.

The Problem

What we have been saying so far is quite theoretical and might even seem to be so far removed from the harsh reality of things that it is not a viable approach to the meaning of love in our present times and society. At least it might seem that way to us who have a rich heritage of "problems" about human sexuality and the relation of one's body to one's self. We only have to recall the heritage of puritanism which has oddly developed into the demeaning of sex rather than its ennoblement. There seem to be ecclesiastical positions of the past and the present which militate against the understanding of sexuality as a good for man. The totality of "morals" itself has often been identified with sex.

On the other hand we have pressures in our culture today which saturate communications with a form of sexuality that is either a vinyl-coated fantasyland or a variation on a theme by Hugh Hefner. This is the other side of the odd polarity—from an angelistic distrust of the body and sexuality to a mechanistic and depersonalized cult of the body without the human implications of love and involvement.

Even before considering the problem, one thing should be kept in mind: the ways and potentialities of human love follow upon the ways and potentialities of human knowing. And as we have already seen, the modes of human knowledge are inextricably, as far as we can tell, united to the senses, to animal ways of knowing. But even though this tie is evident, human knowledge transcends the limitations and boundaries of sense knowledge. As a consequence, man's loving potentialities will be composed—if they are operating in integrated human action—of both sensory and intellectual characteristics. I am a unity; and as an integrated unity I should love.

Human love by definition includes sensual elements. I will love bodily, experiencing warmth, physical attraction, appealing scents, evocative sounds. Moreover, in the love of any other person, I might experience a physical resonance, change in pulse, or physical "well being."

Human love, by definition, will also include elements which transcend the level of sheer physical being. In knowing myself and consequently possessing myself, I will experience the drive to bestow myself to the other or open myself in communication or sacrifice. Moreover, I will also find myself responding to the gift of the other to me, valuing the other's goodness, uniqueness, and irreplaceability.

Thus it would have a disintegrating effect upon my total identity if I were to reduce my ability to love to either angelism or animalism. I am *both:* an animal which transcends its animality. The

105

human manifestation of love, then, will include both realms of human potentialities; and if a human being is to love in an integrated fashion, there will be a correspondence between these two realms. The physical expression of human love, therefore, must be an expression of the totality of human love—if it is to be an authentic act of a total person. The physical action without the integral intention of love causes a bifurcation in the person's identity. My body says something which my person does not mean. It is precisely because I can say something with my body that my bodily actions achieve dignity and meaning beyond the mere functioning of a physical organism.

On the other hand, the intention of "intellectual" love will become barren and desiccated if it is not exhibited by a *sign* of the toal person—whether it be a gift, a word, smile, or sexual intercourse. The intention of love without its manifestation in action is close to being not love at all, but rather an empty velleity.

Consequently, the physical and the spiritual are both aspects of human love. One without the other can result not only in disintegration, but also in alienation from one's very identity. As soon as the body is reduced to something other than a *sign* of the total person, the body becomes a *thing* and the person loses his uniqueness and irreplaceability. Prostitution, promiscuity, and sex-without-the-meaning-of-self-gift are all examples of this alienation and reduction of the human person to a thing.

> This kind of eroticism represents a crippled form of love. The use of such a phrase as I "have *had* this woman" fully exposes the nature of such eroticism. What you "have" you can swap; what you possess you can change. If a man has "possessed" a woman, he can easily exchange her, can "buy" himself another—What a person *is* as such does not count, only how much sex appeal the person has as a possible sexual partner. . . .
>
> And both part empty-handed. In the mutual surrender of love, in the giving and the taking between two people, each one's personality comes into its own. The love impulse breaks through to that layer of being in which

every individual human being no longer represents a "type" but himself alone, not comparable, not replaceable, and possessing all the dignity of his uniqueness. . . . Since love is not directed toward the aspect of the other person which can be "possessed," toward what the other "has"; since true love is rather directed toward what the other "is"—such real love, and it alone, leads to the monogamous attitude. For the monogamous attitude presupposes comprehension of the partner in all his uniqueness and singularity, comprehending the core and the worth of his personality going beyond all bodily and temperamental peculiarities, since these are not unique and singular and can be found in other persons of more or less the same cast. [7]

Human sexuality, which is a sign of the self, becomes alienating and pathological when it is turned into a marketable commodity. And although Frankl's words are not necessarily a priori truths, they do make an interesting comparison to the nubile, *thingified* centerfolds of *Playboy* which is the ultimacy in non-committal sex. Here we have a woman offered, not even as a possible sexual partner, but rather as the object of the safe stare, the tool of a voyeur which can be looked at without the fear of even having to touch her. Whatever may be the pretensions of "sexual liberty" and the sweet life, the fact is evident here: a woman is a product—a multi-million dollar one in fact—and not an irreplaceable human person. It's not that the playboy view of human sexuality is necessarily bad or gross. It's just unintelligent. Especially when so much is at stake with so many potentialities involved. [8]

It is this phenomenon—found not only in our favorite publications, but also in our advertising and various sexual cults—which Rollo May has called the "New Puritanism." May registers an indictment against those contemporary forces that are destroying the fullest potentialities of human love by reducing love to the machine-functioning of the body without reference to the self-transcending personal gift that it symbolizes. In our "liberated" world today, there is certainly no lack of sexual activity and experimentation; this area has been exhausted. "In fact we find just the opposite in the people who come for help: a great deal of talk about sex, a great deal of sexual activity, practically no one complaining of any cultural prohibitions over his going to bed as often or with as many partners as he wishes."[9] What is complained about is the fact that sex seems to have lost its significance, to have become frustrating, to have become mechanized. There is no feeling, no passion, "so much sex and so little meaning or even fun in it."

Although anxiety due to external prohibition has been decreased, there is, May contends, a continual increase in internalized anxiety and guilt. This is an internalized anxiety caused not by cultural or ecclesiastical taboos, but rather by a disintegration of one's identity or a lack of fidelity to one's potentialities. It is like the phenomenon of "intrinsic guilt," as Maslow calls it, which is the "betrayal of one's own inner nature or self."[10] When one's sexuality does not mean anything to the self as a total person, it does not mean anything. It becomes an atrophied human potentiality.

Rollo May mentions another dilemma which has arisen from the proliferation of technique and "how-to-do-it" books. My sexuality becomes an object which is *apart from* me rather than *a part of* me. It is as if I could study it and develop it without entering into a personal confrontation with its meaning. The old mind-body dualism appears again—now in a different form. "Our modern sexual attitudes have a new content, namely full sexual expression, but in the same old puritan form—alienation from the body and feeling, and exploitation of the body as though it were a machine. . . . The victorian person sought to have love without falling into sex; the modern person seeks to have sex without falling into love."[11]

The fact that human sexuality derives its fundamental significance from its meaning as a sign of a self-transcending gift to a unique, irreplaceable person—this fact is unrealized. And sex becomes a banal vacuity. The deepest meaning of eroticism—which is enhanced and enriched by the fact that one's partner is the one who is fully beloved—is missed. And even the physical joys of sexual love are dwarfed to the level of eating bonbons. Sex, May tells us in Huxley's words, is little more than "panting palm to palm," dripping with unrealized and unfulfilling melodrama. A symptom of this is

108

premature monogamy, a state of not being totally committed to the other person, in which sex becomes something to do when you run out of conversation.

> which happens often when the partners have not developed enough in their own right to be interesting very long to each other as persons. It is a strange fact in our society that what goes into building a relationship—the sharing of tastes, fantasies, dreams, hopes for the future and fears from the past—seems to make people more shy and vulnerable than going to bed with each other. They are more wary of the tenderness that goes with psychological and spiritual nakedness than they are of the physical nakedness of sexual intimacy.[12]

Sexual intimacy is not a very difficult thing to do when you come right down to it. Actually it's a fairly common thing. And humans certainly are not alone in possessing the capacity. What is uncommon is what a human being can *do with* and *mean by* sexual communion. What is uncommon is the open intimacy of two free persons giving their total selves to each other.

And these are not the only obstacles before us in trying to form a viable philosophy of human sexuality. Our media do not help. The era of the "Mechanical Bride" is flush upon us. Just check automobile advertising for the flood of images identifying sexuality with power and aggression. The shape, appearance, and even the natural odor of the human body is not only enhanced, but even distorted by canned-beauty-producers. People pay two dollars to have their shoes shined by a topless beauty queen with silicone breasts. The ultimacy of sexual mechanization can be read in the Masters-Johnson Report. And it was reflecting on these phenomena that led Malcolm Muggeridge in his *Esquire* article to opt for the downfall of human sexuality.

> Sex begins in ecstasy, momentarily fusing two separate egos into union with one another and with all life; it ends with a total separation of one ego exclusively occupied with its

own orgasm. Sex as a window onto eternity is a beginning, and it ends in a dark cellar, self-enclosed and boarded with time. Sex begins as the sap rises in a tree to make buds and blossom and leaves and fruit; it ends in Dr. Masters' Sex Report. Sex begins as a mystery out of which come the art, the poetry, the religious delight of successive civilizations; it ends in a laboratory. Sex begins in passion, it comprehends the concepts of both suffering and joy; it ends in a trivial dream of passion which itself soon dissolves into the secrecy of despair and self-gratification. If this indeed be Sex, then *Down With Sex*.[13]

Muggeridge rightly sets the stakes high. But perhaps his conclusion is not necessary if a reflective person can see and remain faithful to his potentialities as a sexual being. And the rewards are great—at least according to men like Fromm, May, and Frankl. Human sexuality rooted in human love can lead to a greater enrichment and fulfillment of the person, a greater self-awareness and sensitivity, a greater ability to give and share in love, and the birth of new selves. Fromm emphasizes the horizons of tenderness, unity, and integration which are found in human love—sexual or otherwise. Frankl speaks of the values, the joys, the salvation which man can find in love. And José de Vinck, himself a married man, sees human sexuality grounded in love as one of the most fulfilling possibilities for man.

By its very nature, the act of love is one whole and continuous ascension; once it has been set in motion, any obstacle, inhibition or slowing down tends to destroy it completely. That is why the taming and control of the senses must take the form, not of scruples within the act itself, but of an adequate orientation prior to it. . . .

Sex rightly used eliminates obsession, for the satisfaction of the natural drive within the norms of reason—that is, including a lavish mutual gift of sensual love—serves not as kindling for a devouring fire, but as a steady and pacifying flame that grows in warmth and quality. Wherever obsession appears, or the fire of passion rises to a dangerous heat, sex is not rightly used. The universal erotomania which is so much part of our present civilization is a certain sign that sex has reached not its full development, but that it is immature... The reason is precisely that sex, instead of being a virtuous habit, has become an end in itself. Instead of remaining a true but secondary reward of love, it has been turned into an absolute religion. . . .

At the times of manifesting sexual love, modesty and reserve are wrong, and so is impatience and greed, for they tend to deprive both partners of their fun, of what was made to be the supreme form of adult play, the best remedy to sadness, isolation, and despair; an act of immense human and divine significance. There is no better time for the singing of psalms than the morning after a night of love.[14]

To achieve this, however, is impossible, if it is not realized that human sexuality derives its deepest meaning and significance from the fact that it is the *sign* of and testimony to self-transcending human love. There are not only psychological foundations for seeing sexual love in this way; there are also the philosophical implications of questioning man who discovers his identity to be more than his sexuality and realizes that he must be faithful to that identity if he is to be himself.

The Resolution

The realization of man's potentialities for human love can only come with the recognition that he is neither angel nor animal, with a loving acceptance of his body as his presence to the world, and with the understanding that human love cannot be reduced to human sexuality—although it can be enhanced by it. Moreover, man must realize that in loving he does not appropriate the beloved, nor does his love find its exhaustion in her alone. His love is rather an open transparence[15] to the beloved, a response to the horizons of value he sees in her, and a free gift of himself to her—and through her, as Fromm would maintain—to humanity.[16] To do this is to affirm the ultimate value of personhood in the cosmos. For it is only because we are persons that we love. It is through our personhood that we are driven, in need, outside of ourselves, so that we may give ourselves to and be united with the other.

> Only love can bring individual beings to their perfect completion, as individuals, by uniting them one with another, because only love takes possession of them and unites them by what lies deepest within them. This is simply a fact of our everyday experience. For indeed, at what moment do lovers come into the most complete possession of themselves if not when they say they are lost in one another?[17]

Man's identity as a knower and a wanter comes to its fullest meaning when he loves, for he is precisely fulfilling himself by "dying" to himself and going out of himself into the world of value and persons. Again we see a resolution to the problem of egoism and altruism. Self-fulfillment is achieved only in self-divestment. Of course, if I were defined and reduced to my body, there would be no resolution. There would be only the immediate fulfillment of my present demands as an organism. In the sexual realm, as in any other human realm, this does not work, because one's personhood is fighting to be realized. And if it is not realized, there ensue only disintegration and alienation from one's very identity.

When a man loves another, he is affirming the very values for which he in his humanity is striving: the fullness of knowledge, of love, and of communion. When he loves, he is testifying to his own identity and his demand to transcend himself, to possess himself, to give himself. This is the root of every man's dignity, uniqueness, irreplaceability. Only I can give myself to another.

And what makes me "want" to love in the first place is the dynamism of personhood and the unconditional drive to know and give. I am prompted by the presence of other persons and the horizon of values which I see in them, in which they partake, but which no *one* of them nor *all* of them exhaust. Personhood, then, drives me outside of myself toward the fuller realization of and union with and affirmation of personhood. Perhaps, then, when a man says he loves, he is saying that he sees the absolute value of person in the beloved, and it is his own participation in personhood which induces him to affirm the value of the other.

> If men on earth, all over the earth, are ever to love one another, it is not enough for them to recognize in one another the elements of a single *something;* they must also, be developing a "planetary" consciousness, become aware of the fact that without loss of their individual identities, they are becoming a single *somebody.* For there is no total love—and this is writ large in the gospel—save that which is in and of the personal.[18]

In conclusion, then, we might say:

a) Man, in his animality, in his contingency, in his need for self-validation, often thinks what "must be done" is to appropriate, to saturate himself with things and people *added on* to himself. However, because of his very identity, such attempts at self-validation and fulfillment of immediate needs only serve to intensify his drive "to do and be something" rather than still it.

b) Upon questioning himself, he finds that his identity actually entails a demand to know himself, possess himself, and transcend himself in an act of free self-gift. His sexuality, if it is to be integrated with this identity, must be a sign of such a gift if it is to have human significance.

c) Experientially, if he truly loves (and even if he does not philosophize about it) he is brought out of himself in a response to the other and the world of values to which the other—in his personhood—testifies.

d) The horizon of values, however, and his ability to love are not exhausted by the beloved. There is a self-transcendence demanded of the couple itself, a testimony to the values of personhood, knowledge, and love. They too must be open to what is "other," to what is value, to what is personal; if they remain closed in on themselves, their love will cease and they will retrogress to encapsulation. This is the road to transcendence through the other. Perhaps this is what Rilke is speaking of when he says, "Lovers . . . I know you touch each other . . . because you feel pure permanence underneath."[19]

THE METAPHYSICS OF LOVE
F. D. Wilhelmsen[28]

What does an existential analysis teach us about the tragic dimension of life? I would suggest that the most cavalier scrutiny of the human condition reveals man as contingent, as finite, as without roots in himself, as lacking the support of the world which is his own, as forever hovering on the brink of nothingness. The death of children, the carrying of coffins, the advent of age, the failure of memory, the cruelty of change, the parting of lovers, the absence of friends, the passing of youth, the knowledge of evil—all these things shake and sunder the being of man. Turn to whomever he might; seek what comfort he can command; and marshal what support he can muster, each man knows that in the final reckoning nothing from without can save him from the groundlessness which is his history and his being. Called in a unique manner to care for the things that are, the man who shoulders his task with heroism and realism does so knowing well enough that he is but contingent, that those depending on him depend on a being fragile and without roots.

This is the famous "encounter with nothingness" probed by Heidegger. Nothing is not a thing nor is it a function; it is but a failure in the very heart of our being—a failure promising only the grave. Nor does it suffice, insists existentialist philosophy, to point out the truth that all things die and that death is but the mark of radical contingency of the universe of creatures. All things die, but only man *has to die.* . . . Man knows his contingency. Since man is a knowing-being, the knowledge of his contingency is one with his person. No man is really human who has not faced the meaning of his own death, and only those men who face it daily are fully human.

Man is the paradox in being. Perpetually falling into the nothing, glowering from without and erupting as a hideous void from within, man nonetheless fails to achieve his own failure. He does not cease to be, although everything which is a part of the tragic dimension of existence cries out demanding his annihilation . . . Men die, but they never experience death. Whatever it be that lies beyond death lies beyond history. Death, therefore, hides itself from philosophical *experience*. The best we can do is to insist that an existential analysis points up the intolerable and yet curiously bracing truth that man is forever threatened by annihilation and yet never is annihilated, is forever menaced by non-being and yet continues to be.

Experiencing the possibility of non-being as the enemy of his being, man senses his finiteness as transcendence. Hunting for an absolute ground to his being, man opens doors and each one of them leads nowhere. Yet he still opens doors. He even does so when he does nothing more than hang on grimly to the shadow of his being, as do those pitiful wrecks of humanity who populate our asylums, driven there by anxiety, haunted by the specter of the facelessness and silence of non-being. They too continue to be. Each man, therefore, seeks a way out of the insecurity which is one with life. Each man seeks to transcend his own transcendence. Things below man are finite and contingent, but only man is driven both to face finiteness and attempt to shake off its sting. Scratching forever in the soil of being, the race is destined to track down a place within which humanity can take root and there flourish within the shadow of the absolute . . . Man demands a certain and non-failing ground of being. Humanity makes the demand but not in the sense that the absolute is commanded by the demand; were this so, the facts marshalled above would be phantoms: we would have found a more comfortable world than the one in which we are. Man demands the absolute as the term of his own transcending—the term is not dragooned into obedience by the call of man. The search for beatitude does not guarantee its fulfillment. Man calls for the absolute in the sense that his being is a being-towards-being, finiteness tending to the infinite in the language of Vico, a thirsting for immortal life in the terms of Unamuno, desirous of God in Aquinas, the restless soul in the wisdom of Augustine.

Here the tragic sense of life meets the ecstatic. Falling into nothing even while he strives to be, experiencing himself essentially as ontological poverty, man nonetheless must give of himself to the world of things and most especially to the world of persons. The being of man is . . .*structurally a being with others*. Revealed in the first instance in communication, which is a demand to share meaning with another person; experienced in care, which is the contingent watch over the contingent, the ecstatic drive in man reaches its culmination in love. When a man loves, his being now is a being-for-another. The lover lives literally in the being of the beloved. This is the metaphysics latent in the beautiful phrase, common to many languages, "being in love."

That love is an authentic human experience, that the being of man is achieved only in love, and that therefore the being of man is structurally open to love, are all most forcefully pointed by an analysis of the negation of love. The negation of love is a self-destroying experience, as are the negations of care and courage . . . If love is the free giving of the person to another person, the opposite of love is the attempt to appropriate the being of another to oneself. At the root of every such appropriation there lies the drive in man to conquer his own indigence, to overcome his own ontological poverty. Experiencing himself as limited and finite, the unauthentic human being tries to make up the lack by a gathering into his being the being of another. If we scrutinize this act carefully, we discover that it involves a vicious contradiction, a metaphysical violation. Hoping to make the being of another a being *for* himself in order that he might fill up what is lacking in his own existence, the unauthentic man ends by turning his own being into a *being-for-the-appropriated*. Thus the miser begins by relating himself to money and ends by being defined by the very money he has appropriated: in a profound sense he has become little more than a being-for-money. He thus becomes the slave of his own conquest. Here is the irony involved in every failure to respect the irreducibility and the dignity of the being of another thing or person: the attempt to make another's being exclusively a being-for-me ends in my making my being a being-for-that-other. This is what I mean by a self-defeating experience. Ontological poverty is not overcome; it is simply accentuated.

The ecstatic and the tragic meet in a paradox which is one with the being of man. The desire to give and the desire to be

117

fulfilled, the need to throw myself away and the need to be sheltered, are one with human life; logically these drives are opposed; existentially they *are* the being of man. To say all this is but to say that man is not a complete person until he has been loved in and by the act of a Person to whom he can give himself freely and who will freely give him—rather *be* for him—the anchor in being that man so desperately needs. . . .

This being that man is through participation is not sealed and closed within itself: it is open—it is destined both to expend itself upon the universe of being and to find therein or in its Source the completion it so desperately needs. It would appear that the human person were better described, not in terms of incommunicability, but in terms of communication and even communion. The person is not circumscribed in being or described adequately in knowledge in terms of the sealed ego. Personality is not constituted by an "I": Personality is constituted by a "we."

1. Jean-Paul Sartre, *No Exit*, translated by Stuart Gilbert. (New York: Vintage Books, 1946), p. 47.

2. Viktor Frankl, *Man's Search For Meaning* (New York: Washington Square Press, 1963), pp. 58-59.

3. Jean-Paul Sartre, *Being and Nothingness*, translated by Hazel Barnes. (New York: Citadel, 1965), p. 340.

4. Erich Fromm, *The Art of Loving* (New York: Bantam, 1956), p. 17. See also *Man For Himself* for further developments of Fromm's theories and their relation to ethics.

5. Viktor Frankl, *The Doctor and the Soul* (New York: Bantam, 1967), pp. 106-107.

6. *Ibid.*, 107.

7. *Ibid.*, pp. 115, 116, 117, 118, passim.

8. These reflections are made just to see some of the implications of the "Playboy Philosophy," concerning which Hefner has written much. Reprints of his articles can be had from HMH Publishing Co. There is also a series of round-table discussions in which Hefner defends his approach as one which does not necessarily involve objectification and alienation of the body.

9. Rollo May, "Antidotes for the New Puritanism," *Saturday Review,* March 26, 1966, p. 19. A section of this article is also reprinted in the paperback book of essays, *Sex in America*, ed. by H. A. Grunwald (New York: Bantam, 1964), pp. 161-165.

10. Abraham Maslow, *Toward a Psychology of Being* (Princeton: Insight-Van Nostrand, 1962), p. 181. "If this essential core [inner nature] of the person is frustrated, denied, or suppressed, sickness results . . ." Cf. also 182: "Intrinsic guilt is the consequence of betrayal of one's own inner nature or self, a turning off the path to self-actualization, and is essentially justified self-disapproval." See also the foreword by Fromm in *Man For Himself* (Greenwich, Conn: Premier Books, 1965).

11. May, *op. cit.*, p. 19.

12. *Ibid.*, p. 21.

13. Malcom Muggeridge, "Down with Sex!" from *Esquire* (Feb. 1966), p. 74.

14. José De Vinck, *The Virtue of Sex* (New York: Hawthorn Books, 1966), pp. 228, 229, 237.

15. See, in this connection, Sidney M. Jourard, *The Transparent Self* (Princeton: Insight-Van Nostrand, 1964), Chapter four.

16. Fromm, *The Art of Loving*, chapters two and four.

17. Pierre Teilhard de Chardin, *Hymn of the Universe* (New York: Harper and Row, 1961), p. 145.

18. *Ibid.*, p. 89.

19. Rainer Marie Rilke, *Duinic Elegies.*

20. F. D. Wilhelmsen, *The Metaphysics of Love* (New York: Sheed and Ward, 1962), pp. 17-24, passim. Reprinted by permission of Sheed and Ward, Inc.

The books listed at the end of chapters four and six for the most part have sections dealing with the meaning of human love. There are also countless films *(La Strada, Nights of Cabiria, L'Avventura, Woman of the Dunes, Elvira Madigan, Who's Afraid of Virginia Woolf?,* and *Faces),* plays, and novels which concretely bring out both the potentialities and pathologies of love.

De Beauvoir, *The Second Sex,* tr. H. M. Parshley. New York: Bantam, 1961. This is a philosophical, psychological, and historical study of the relationship between man and woman with overtones of Sartrian interpretation.

De Rougemont, Denis. *Love in the Western World.* New York: Doubleday Anchor, 1956. A well articulated and expansive treatment of a nihilating romantic love which has played an important part in western culture.

Frankl, Viktor. *The Doctor and the Soul.* New York: Bantam, 1965. Already mentioned, this book has an excellent chapter touching upon human sexuality and love.

Johann, Robert. *The Meaning of Love.* Glen Rock, N. J.: Deus Books, 1966. A good philosophical treatment, Thomistic in tone, heavy-going at times, but greatly reqarding, this book has later been followed by *Building the Human* (New York: Herder and Herder, 1968), a series of stimulating essays which more fully represents Johann's present thought.

Jourard, Sidney. *The Transparent Self.* Princeton: Van Nostrand-Insight, 1964. A psychologist's new and refreshing approach to the meaning and practice of interpersonal relations.

Lepp, Ignace. *The Psychology of Loving.* New York: Mentor Omega, 1963. Concentrating on the pathologies of human love and sexuality, it is an interesting study by a priest-psychologist.

Nedoncelle, Maurice. *Love and the Person.* New York: Sheed and Ward, 1966. Covers a broad range of approaches, personalistic.

Nietzsche, Friedrich. *The Philosophy of Nietzsche.* New York: Modern Library, 1954. A good, inexpensive edition, this book contains *Thus Spake Zarathustra* and *Beyond Good and Evil.* If read with as open a mind as possible, it can be a jangling, envigorating, and challenging experience.

Rand, Ayn. *For the New Intellectual.* New York: Signet, 1961. A sometime disciple of Nietzsche, Hobbes, and Macchiavelli (to some extent), in both her novels and this work she manages to call into question many aprioris.

Sartre, Jean-Paul. *Being and Nothingness* (cited previously). This work is worth mentioning again, for its fully developed theory of intersubjectivity which challenges most honestly and ruthlessly many of the positions held in this book. See also *No Exit.*

Teilhard de Chardin, Pierre. *Hymn of the Universe.* New York: Harper and Row, 1961. Reflective meditations, pensees, and mystical prayers on man-as-unfolding to The Other.

Wilhelmsen. F. D. *The Metaphysics of Love.* New York: Sheed and Ward, 1962. This book, like many in the bibliography, is mentioned because it might not be known as well as other familiar works. It is a profound treatment of the ambiguities of human nature and an attempt at a resolution of these ambiguities with a philosophy of love. The second half of the book, however, is exclusively concerned with some recent Spanish philosophers.

Chapter Six

The Unfolding Of Open Potentialities

The Human Soul

"Much ado about nothing," he thought. For nothing: this life had been given him for nothing, he was nothing and yet he would not change; he was as he was made... He yawned: he had finished the day, and he had also finished with his youth. Various tried and proved rules of conduct had already discreetly offered him their services: disillusioned epicureanism, smiling tolerance, resignation, flat seriousness, stoicism—all the aids whereby a man may savor, minute by minute, like a connoisseur, the failure of a life. He took off his jacket and began to undo his necktie. He yawned again as he repeated to himself: "It's true, it's true: I have attained the age of reason."[1]

Jean-Paul Sartre

Death is the most profound and significant fact of life: it lifts the very last of mortals above the greyness and banality of life. And only the fact of death puts the question of life's meaning in all its depth. Life in this world has meaning only because there is death... Meaning is linked with ending. And if there were no end, if in our world there was evil and endlessness of life, there would be no meaning to life whatever. Meaning lies beyond the bounds of this

*closed world, and the discovery of meaning presupposes an
ending in this world.*[2]

Nicolai Berdyaev

*Death reaches down to the depths of being only in the
measure that it is not repose but realization. In life,
everything that is attained or consummated thereby
becomes like death. Nothing completed can live. To move
towards realization, therefore, is to move towards death.*[3]

Gabriel Marcel

The human person is something like a kernel, which, in order to
realize its meaning, must burst out of its own encapsulation. Unlike
the kernel, however, the human person has something to say about
its encapsulation and self-realization. In human psychophysical
development, that moment of "saying something" begins at the
moment of questioning when man tries to liberate himself from the
necessities of environment and historicity. His very first option arises
with the decision whether to question or not. He does not have to
respond to the invitation of questioning, but once he has, he has
committed himself to the philosophical enterprise and the implications it will have for his life.

The person is then confronted with his identity as a questioner
and the consequent course of action that a questioner must take.
This is the moment of philosophy: and since his drives to know, to
do something, to *be* someone are all unconditionally open, the
moment will never cease. Try to "put them off" as he may, his
personhood and identity cannot be put off. Like it or not, sooner or
later, he must do something with himself, for to be a person is
precisely to experience a demand to do something with oneself, to
be free, to know, and to love. To be such a thing and to have the
potentialities for such actions is to be human; and that by which I
am human and able to do "human" things as a unified agent I will
call the human soul.

When we see a thing that grows, reproduces, reacts, and adapts
itself all for the good of the whole, for one dynamic purpose of the
organism, we can see the need for a total organizing principle of all

these activities. Such a principle of living activities is frequently called a living "soul"—not some ghost within the thing, but rather the dynamic unifying principle of the whole.

Vegetative living organisms have the basic internal dynamism directed toward the enhancement and realization of the total organism. Growth, repair, reproduction, irritability all are direction-oriented for the sake of the total unity which is on its own working for its own good. In the case of animals, not only are there activities of growth, reproduction, irritability, and adaptation, but there are also the dynamic operations of cognition and appetite on the internal and external sense levels. And all of these are also directed toward the actualization of the total animal. The unifying principle in this case can be called the animal soul.

With respect to man, however, there are not only the activities mentioned above, but there are other activities which, as we have seen, transcend the limitations of those mentioned in the case of sub-human organisms. These precisely human activities—intellection, love, free-choice, and self-possession—are also ordered for the good of the man as a unity. And again, the unifying principle of all these human activities (including the vegetative and sensorial activities) is the human soul. It is specifically a "human" soul because it is precisely that about me by which I operate as an individual human with specifically human potentialities and powers. It is that not only by which I live and sense but also that by which I am open to the world in knowledge and love. "Soul" is a way of naming the fact of what I am and what I am able to do as *this* type of being—which other types of beings can not do.

Amplifying Note

In Catholic theology and philosophy, the soul has often been spoken of in the context of the matter-form (hylemorphic) theory. That *by which* I am precisely *this* type, or the way I am as a man (as opposed to a tree, for instance) is the substantial form (the internal constitutive structure), which in the case of a human being is the soul. "Form is nothing more or less than the fact that the thing is the way it is: this kind of being, resulting from the adequate action of an efficient cause upon a properly disposed material cause. It is not a thing separate from the being itself, like an extrinsic cause. Like a material cause, it causes not by doing anything, but by being."[4] In other words, I am this sort of form (human), having a human nature with human potentialities. Matter and form simply refer to the fact that this designated quantity of matter is now existing as *this kind* of being. Form is not a thing; it does not come and go. It simply begins and ceases accordingly as the being is or is not this kind of being. Now this kind of being that I am happens to manifest living, knowing, and loving operations which are distinctive to *my kind* of being. That by which I am this particular kind of being is the human substantial form which we call the soul.[5]

The reason why we have taken this digression is that, after having talked about the questions of identity and action, we might want to discuss the root or basis or principle of that identity and those actions. I am a unique occurrence of the human soul, with unique abilities, aspirations, and a unique life project. And the question has consistently struck the minds of men: "What happens with the cessation of that life project, when life seems only to issue in death?" Or put another way: what happens to the radical basis of my identity, an identity which has been formed precisely through the operations of knowing, loving, and choosing—all of which we came to know as being non-quantifiable, irreplaceable, and non-material.

This is the problem of human life, death, and immortality; and it is a problem which has not been limited only to the ruminations of philosophers or professional theologians.

But because being here amounts to so much, because all
this here and now so fleeting seems to require us and strangely
concerns us. Us the most fleeting of all. Just once,
Everything only for once. Once and no more. And we, too
once. And never again. But this
having been once, though only once
having been once on earth—can it ever be cancelled?[6]

Am I a coiled spring, wound up for one useless thrust going nowhere, or am I a self that never can be cancelled. The question of death and man's ultimate meaning cannot be avoided, even though we might try to ignore it. Philosophical reckoning cannot be put off. Blaise Pascal puts the matter provocatively:

> 168. *Diversion.* As men are not able to fight against death, misery, ignorance, they have taken it into their heads, in order to be happy, not to think of them at all.

> 169. Despite these miseries, man wishes to be happy, and only wishes to be happy, and cannot wish not to be so. But how will he set about it? To be happy he would have to make himself immortal; but, not being able to do so, it has occurred to him to prevent himself from thinking about death.[7]

Think about it we must, for as Simone de Beauvoir has reminded us, we begin to die with the moment of birth. But before coming to a reflective analysis of the possible meanings of death, we might first consider two of the major philosophical arguments offered to prove the immortality of the soul.

The Metaphysical Argument

If an organism has operations which depend intrinsically upon matter and its operations fail to transcend quantitative and extensional characteristics, it seems quite evident that, once the material conditions of operation have ceased to be functional, the principle of those activities has no reason to exist. Thus vegetation, physical growth, irritability, and reproductive functions—all intrinsically material—have a material principle of dynamic unity which has no reason to exist (and could not exist) without the physical conditions involved. Similarly, in the case of sense knowledge which is tied down to the limitations and conditions of matter intrinsically, the principle of animal appetitive and cognitive functions would seem to have no reason for existing once the animal functions have ceased.

In the case of man, however, a unique problem arises. In our previous analyses of knowledge and love, we saw that these operations, although needing material conditions as far as we can tell (sense knowledge, phantasms, the functioning of the brain), manifest qualities and characteristics intrinsically independent of matter. I can know universal ideas, omitting precisely the concrete and material, as I express and know the transcending, non-representational, non-material aspects. I can make truth, justice, goodness all objects of my knowing and striving, in which I am open to *all*, whether sensorially expressed or not. I have the ability to reflect back upon myself as a totality, to think upon my thinking.

Now *I* do these things (as opposed to experiencing my body doing these things), and I have the power to do these things. Those powers, in order to have objects and operations which are free of material limitations, must be immaterial in themselves (even though extrinsically, in order to be manifested in a living physical body, they must have the external-extrinsic conditions of matter).

> Scientific objectivity postulates subjective consciousness, that is, self-knowledge and self-apprehension. Such reflection, again, postulates simplicity. If the subject were essentially a composite, it could never arrive at apprehending its own self as a whole. At the most, one part would perhaps grasp another part. That is precisely where the difference lies between the body, which is material, and the subject, which is spiritual. The hand may grasp anything except itself, whereas the subject is aware of itself as a self without stepping out of itself. In order to reflect in this manner, the subject must rise above the body whose corporeality would constitute an obstacle; it must be intrinsically detached from the multiplicity of parts it vivifies, and turn upon itself at one indivisible point. While being related to space through the body, the subject as a spirit is not subject to space. Total reflection, a condition of scientific knowledge, implies simplicity, which in turn is the pledge of immortal life.[8]

128

That by which I do all the activities previously named, including self-reflection, which are precisely human things, is the human soul. The soul, in order to be the principle of these powers and activities of knowing and loving, must be immaterial, free from the conditions of matter, and capable of perduring on its own if the material conditions should cease to be.

This is about all that one can say about the life of the soul after it is separated from the body and ceases to exist in conjunction with extrinsic material conditions. It will certainly be existing in a different mode, and knowledge and love will have to take place in a different manner than it does with a body and senses. Moreover, it would seem that the life of a soul separated from the body will be an unnatural state of affairs. But we do not have the data to say anything more. All that we can really say, we have said:

a) I *do* "immaterial" things: know and love in ways that transcend the conditions and limitations of materiality.

b) The powers of intellect and will by which I do these things must in turn be immaterial in order to enable me to do immaterial things.

c) That *by which* I am precisely human, capable of doing *human* things, must likewise be immaterial—hence, not subject to material or physical death and corruption.

The Phenomenological Argument

Another possible approach might be found in an analysis of the drives to know and to love. In our experience we realize that these drives have an unrestricted quality to them: they transcend all cultural and historical idiosyncrasies; they are not limited to any particular object. They also have an unconditional aspect to them: they are not exhausted like physical appetites; they do not become satiated or satisfied when particular goals are achieved. In that they are open to all that is knowable and lovable, they seem never to be filled to capacity. Their unrestricted nature is the very thing which keeps them going. We never come to acquisitive, cognitive, or even appropriative homeostasis. There is always more. Pathologically, there is always more to get—more money, more land, more power. Authentically, there is always more to give—more openness, more dedication, more desire to be more deeply *one* with another or with the world.

Having considered these drives, at this point a critical option must be made: if man, at the heart of his identity, involves an unconditional drive toward the fullest actualization of his powers to know and love and if as a matter of fact these unconditional drives are never experienced as having *arrived* at their fullest actualization, then the very meaning of man—if he ceases to exist at the moment of physical death—in its most fundamental identity, is radically absurd.

And this is the option: man is fundamentally absurd, or his meaning is fundamentally meaningful. If there is not a form of life after death which transcends the limitations of our existence as we experience it now, and if there is no ultimate realization of man's identity as an openness to unconditional knowledge and love, then human reality is radically absurd. Sartre, I believe, makes this painfully clear at the end of *Being and Nothingness*.

> Every human reality is a passion in that it projects losing itself so as to found being and by the same stroke to constitute the In-itself which escapes contingency by being its own foundation, the *Ens-causa-sui,* which religions call God. Thus the passion of man is the reverse of Christ, for man loses himself as man in order that God may be born. But the idea of God is contradictory and we lose ourselves in vain. Man is a useless passion.[9]

If there is no life after physical death (and ultimately, if there is no unconditional response to man's drives of knowledge and love), then man is a useless passion. The *to be* of man is to-be-frustrated.

To make the option for human reality radically meaningful, on the other hand, is to affirm the existence of man after death. Since his human potentialities are not ultimately fulfilled in the present human condition, in order for these potentialities to be radically meaningful, they (and their subject) must perdure after death.

The *option,* then, is quite critically important. And if one opts for absurdity he must not only explain away the flashes of meaning, he must also *live* that absurdity. It will make no difference whether one is a solitary drunkard or a leader of nations.[10] If, on the other hand, meaning is opted for, the maker of the option must not only confront the absurdity in human life as a manifestation of freedom's ambiguities, but he must also *live* the meaning of his identity.

The Meanings of Death

Since, however, we do not have any experiential knowledge of a life after death and therefore cannot really say much about it, it might then be best to speak about the meaning of human life and thereby indirectly come to a reflective understanding of its cessation.

First of all, as a living totality, I experience the dynamism toward fulfillment and actualization of my drives to know and love. Moreover, as a total subject, a self, I experience a drive toward the full realization of all my potentialities as a man. I want to be all that I am capable of being; and I am not necessarily aware of what its limit might be. As Rahner has rather poetically put it, "Man is limitless reference to the infinite mystery of fullness. There is no point in my life at which I might stop and say, 'Everything that I have to do or ever wanted to do is now achieved in fullness."[11] As Marcel said in his quote at the beginning of this chapter, "Nothing completed can live."[12] As long as you have life, the forward dynamism remains. "The tendency to actualize itself is the motive which sets the organism going: it is the *drive* by which the organism is moved."[13] As long as there is life, there is process. "Life is here conceived not as an *immanent* but as a *self-transcending* process. It does not merely tend to preserve a given state, but also points beyond its status quo."[14] All of this is to say, in the words of Carl Rogers, "The organism has one basic tendency and striving—to actualize, maintain, and enhance the experiencing organism."[15]

I have seen, however, that I am a unique kind of organic unity, with powers and potentialities far surpassing the conditions of a physical organism. And my "one basic tendency" includes the fulfillment of my meaning as a person and a questioner. By my relentless questioning, I strive for some self-actualizing ultimate response to my question. And whether this response is made or not, the demand to "go forward" remains.

I must ask myself what the meaning of this insight might be. Like the organism, spoken of by psychologists above, I have a dynamism toward fuller growth and actualization. But I am a questioning organism which can also take its direction into its own hands. I am a project-forming organism, and the project is the direction and meaning of my own growth and life-process. As a self-possessed organism I can define myself and the horizons of my possibilities. Consequently, no matter what else death may mean, it is the cessation of my project-formation, of my self-definition. I can define myself as fifty-thousand dollars a year, as a reputation, as a split-level suburban home, as an income-tax bracket. I can make something of myself—a name, a price-tag, a car. I make the horizons of my own meaning—whether it be the scope of my body, my things, or my openness and fidelity to knowledge and love. What is most interesting here is that if I define myself by my physicality or my body or things, these very things will cause the actual incompleteness of my free project, since we at least know that they cannot transcend the meaning of the here and now.

But if my horizon is precisely *open-ended* and unfolding, self-transcending, questioning and demanding ultimate response in knowledge and love, what can physical death possibly do to these spatio-temporal transcending phenomena? Can death actually mean a cessation of love's permanence, of a project which is open to that which is precisely beyond the limitations and conditions of quantity, materiality, and physicality? This is a question I must ask myself as a philosopher. But before trying to come to a complete answer to it, perhaps I ought to consider some of the other alternative positions concerning death itself.

The Naturalist's Approach

One possible response to the problem of death might be offered by a humanist or a naturalist. Death for him seems to be one of the most difficult problems to confront without hopelessly destroying the worth and ultimate significance of the individual. It would be a radical form of impersonalism, to say the least, to maintain that man (the individual) is offered up on the "slaughtering block of history." And yet this is often the case if we are to consider, liberally oriented as we might be, that man has no aspirations and no meaning other than the immediacy of the present and the inevitability of death. If, as Freud has said, "the goal of all life is death,"[16] then life itself, in our most honest moments, could have only a sourness to it. Should I bear up to the sourness in an offering of myself to the species or the race, itself nothing more than an abstractive combination of other meaningless selves like myself?

Even in facing up to these problems, most naturalists would refuse to look for what might be seen as a philosophical palliative—the warm blanket of an afterlife. Moreover, and rightly so, they would balk before fleeing from the contingencies of this world into the promising securities of the next. About all that a naturalist-humanist can do is to face up to the harsh realities of life and live it as well as possible.

One of the major points of the *Humanist Manifesto* seems to be a devout wish for man, rather than a full recognition of the existential situation. "Religious humanism considers the complete realization of human personality to be the end of man's life and seeks its development and fulfillment in the here and now."[17] But what could possibly be the fulfillment of the human person, if at death his self-project ceases with his physicality, if he is indeed a "death-oriented" dynamism?

W. T. Stace seems to be a bit more realistic in facing up to the implications of total annihilation upon death when he suggests that we live lives of quiet resignation (desperation?) to our hard fate: "To be genuinely civilized means to be able to walk straightly and to live honorably without the props and crutches of one or another of the childish dreams which have so far supported man. That such a life is likely to be ecstatically happy I will not claim. But that it can be lived in quiet content, accepting resignedly what cannot be helped . . . this is what I would maintain."[18] Quiet content and resignation, however, would hardly give rise to the expectations and desires that humanists profess—the dignity of every individual, the pursuit of excellence and truth, the learning of freedom, and the thrust toward the fulfillment of human life. Nonetheless, this is what we are to strive for, even though there is no ultimate meaning and term to the striving. It is not necessary to look for a crutch or a security; but it is necessary to satisfy the demands of the intellect when I ask myself, *why?*

This is not to say that I can learn nothing from the humanist's conception of human life. Quite to the contrary, he offers some important suggestions toward purifying one's notion of an "afterlife":

> a) a rejection of the total man-nature dualism;
> b) a rejection of the notion that a concern for the next world justifies a rejection of this one;
> c) a refusal to embark on a flight from man's contingency into a world of supernaturalism discontinuous with the natural.

These are important considerations to make in one's own philosophical approach to the problem of death, even though the humanist-materialist solution seems wanting in its totality: making ungrounded and overly optimistic demands upon man who is condemned to the futility of directionless aspiration.

The Approach of Some Existentialists

It seems at times as if it is precisely the rampant optimism of the humanist that goads the existentialist into his most profound fulminations about the meaning of man-condemned-to-death. It also seems, moreover, that it is a man like Sartre or Camus who most honestly faces up to the meaning of death when there is no transcendent and no self-transcending, even though they do not offer us the psychological support of "living the good and noble life." In *Being and Nothingness,* as we have seen, Sartre is ruthlessly honest about it. "Man is a useless passion."[19] He is useless because his drives far exceed the reality before him. There is no transcendent, there is no ground of value outside of himself, there is no ultimate response to his unconditional questioning and questing. He is looking for a fantasy, the *causa-sui,* the absolute, the synthetic *en-soi-pour-soi;* and this is a metaphysical impossibility. Hence, all human actions are meaningless in content and, if we should try to give them meaning, we will be falling victims to the "spirit of seriousness."

> Existential psychoanalysis is going to reveal to man the real goal of his pursuit, which is being as a synthetic fusion of the in-itself with the for-itself; existential psychoanalysis is going to acquaint man with his passion . . . Many men, in fact, know that the goal of their pursuit is being; and to the extent that they possess this knowledge, they refrain from appropriating things for their own sake and try to realize the symbolic appropriation of their being-in-itself. But to the extent that this attempt still shares in the spirit of seriousness and that these men can still believe that their mission of effecting the existence of the in-itself-for-itself is written in things, they are condemned to despair; for they discover at the same time that all human activities are equivalent . . . and that all are on principle doomed to failure. Thus it amounts to the same thing whether one gets drunk alone or is a leader of nations. If one of these activities takes precedence over the other, this will not be because of its real goal but because of the degree of consciousness which it possesses of its ideal goal; and in this case it will be the quietism of the solitary drunkard which will take precedence over the vain agitation of the leader of nations.[20]

Here is set up the most fully consistent position on man-without-transcendence.

For a man like Camus, on the other hand, death is a fury to be confronted, a source of dread, an ultimate absurdity capping off an absurd existence. As opposed to Sartre's nausea-filled resignation, however, Camus suggests that man enter into a metaphysical revolt against the ultimate limitation of death by affirming life even in the face of its meaningless end. "Human insurrection, in its exalted and tragic forms, is only, and can only be, a prolonged protest against death, a violent accusation against the universal death penalty."[21] Even in the face of an ultimately meaningless existence, man demands meaning and insists upon reasons for living. "He rejects the consequences implied by death. If nothing lasts, then nothing is justified; everything that dies is deprived of meaning."[22]

Here, in the case of Camus and Sartre, we have a much more rigorous and tenaciously honest confrontation with the meaning of death as the ultimate negation of life, of the human project. And harsh as the implications may be, we must face up to at least the possibility that all human actions take on a futility in the face of ultimate annihilation. More precisely, we should be open to the following insights:

a) If man's horizon and meaning is death, what meaning do man and human action really have?

b) Consequently, one must refuse to accept "rose-colored" promises in the face of death's inevitable prospect.

c) In any approach to man's meaning, the ambiguities of freedom and human ambiguities cannot be ignored.

d) Death cannot be rationalized away or given meaning within the context of "the human race." It might work for the species, but it can hardly be more than a ruse for the individual's "why".

Keeping these points in mind, however, it seems that many data of human life are still left out of this "existential" approach to death. Most basically it rests upon the option (or postulate, in the case of Sartre) that there is not a transcendent ground of meaning, and that man's efforts to transcend himself are futile. Moreover, this approach does have a rather difficult time explaining the manifold areas of meaning in human life.

The Religious Dualism Approach

A third alternative has been offered by *some* men who are aware of a supernatural dimension of reality. Death in this worldview often becomes something of a bludgeon, a threat of god along with the threat of hell, a warning to keep us on a straight and narrow path, hidden from the appeals of this world by supernatural blinders. *This* life and the *next* life are seen as two mutually exclusive and discontinuous lines in which we sacrifice the rewards of one for the promises of the other. We should not enjoy this life too much, or we might forget about the next. This life is a pilgrimage, rather than a project. "This world really *is* a vale of tears, I think the greatest scourge to befall this earth is man, and I wish to escape his sickening handiwork. The thought of death and the assurance of divine mercy is the Catholic's consolation in this life."[23]

Here we have a radical dualism involving a flight from contingency and the human situation. We might be able to see it even in some of our own statements: "my reward will come in the next life"; "If there is no heaven and hell, we have certainly gypped ourselves in this life." Thus we not only demean this world, we become slaves to the next.[24]

Amid the drawbacks, however, there are also some critically important considerations:

a) Man is deeply oriented toward the transcendent, and without values that at least transcend the encapsulated self, human life can only be seen as "nasty, brutish, and short."

b) Man, ultimately enclosed upon himself, is a futility. But the major implication that remains should be forcefully questioned: that the best Christian cannot be the best humanist, that this life must be negated for the sake of the next, that a supernaturalist cannot be a naturalist. As opposed to this position, could it not be possible that one must fully be a son of man in order to realize one's potentialities as a son of God?

So far, we have seen three possibilities. All of these have important points to offer, all have "gaps" in accounting for some data, and all have implicit dualisms. The question then is before us: is there some way to conceive the meaning of human death which will be,

a) a rejection of the natural-supernatural radical dualism;

b) a rejection of the this-world, next-world opposition;

c) a radically involved concern for this life;

d) a consistency in facing up to the ambiguities of human life;

e) a refusal to accept philosophical palliatives or theological escapes;

f) an insistence upon the personal and species-wide human project;

g) a recognition of the dignity of man and the implications of that dignity. Seeing man as radically and fundamentally open, process-oriented, and purposeful.

Man as Openness to the Fullness of Being

We might begin to search for a solution on the same ground from which many humanist-philosophers and psychologists start. Some examples: Erich Fromm insists upon the absolute demand for love in a man's life, a love which transcends not only the individual and the particular couple, but also extends to the entire human species. He recognizes the ambiguities of the human condition, calling it the awareness of one's "separateness" which must be overcome if human fulfillment is to be achieved.[25] These "demands," he maintains, are not imposed by some external source; rather they are human exigencies, springing from the very being and identity of man. Man in his nature is driven outside of himself.

John Dewey calls for a "common faith" of religiousness which involves the self-transcendence of the individual who dedicates himself to an ideal not reducible to himself and which leads himself outside of himself.[26] One of the fundamental psychological principles of Rollo May is that "all existing persons have the need and the possibility of going out from their centeredness to participate in other beings."[27] Gordon Allport claims that psychology itself must be wholly committed to the "entire course of becoming—leaving out no shred of evidence and no level of development."[28] In short, man must be open to the fullest realization of his potentialities as one who is directed outside of himself to others, to the future, to value. Finally, Abraham Maslow offers this observation:

> We can now certainly assert that at least a reasonable, theoretical, and empirical case has been made for the presence within the human being of a tendency toward, or need for growing in the direction that can be summarized in general as self-actualization . . . i.e., he has within him a pressure toward unity of personality, toward spontaneous expressiveness, toward full individuality and identity, toward seeing the truth rather than being blind, toward being creative, toward being good, etc. That is, the human being is so constructed that he presses toward fuller and fuller being, and this means pressing toward what most people would call good values, toward serenity, kindness, courage, honesty, love, unselfishness, and goodness . . .
>
> Man demonstrates *in his own nature* a pressure toward fuller and fuller Being, more and more perfect actualization of his humanness in exactly the same naturalistic sense that an acorn may be said to be "pressing toward" being an oak tree, or that a tiger may be observed to "push toward" being tigerish, or a horse toward being equine.[29]

As in the case of the other men mentioned, man is seen by Maslow as a dynamism, a drive, a process, even a "pressurized drive" toward the fullness of human realization.

What remains for us to reflect upon, therefore, is precisely what gives the "process" meaning and direction, what "fullest self-actualization" could possibly mean. One thing is rather immediately evident: the deepest meaning of process, growth, and self-actualization is most often spoken of in terms of man's seeming insatiable and unconditional drives to know what is knowable and love what is lovable. If man is to be fulfilled, it must be in terms of these potentialities and drives. And if this is the case, the nagging prodding of the existentialists must be kept in mind. Without a direction, a purpose, a ground, and a fulfillment to these drives, the meaning of man is ultimately useless.

In the light of these reflections, then, what might we further say about the meaning of life and death? To be more specific: if human life is a pressure toward fuller and fuller being, if it is a process of becoming what I can become, if it is a growth toward self-actualization, if it is directional, if it is the developmental realization of one's ability to open oneself to knowledge and love and self-possession, then what is death? The evidence points to one overwhelming conclusion: death is the *cessation of becoming,* the finalization of project and process. My process is completed; my project is realized. At this point, *I* am either annihilated (and the whole project becomes a futile joke) or only my *becoming* stops. Ceasing to become, to grow, to proceed (all conditionally dependent upon the factors of spatio-temporal location and materiality) I now *begin to be* what in my life-project I have created myself freely to be, what I have brought to fruition, what I have proceeded *to.*

Thus the most important issue of human life is the nature of the freely creative project which I have formed in growth and culminated in death. Considered from this perspective, there really is no discontinuity between "this" life and "the next" life. There is only the one life of the one self, divisible into project and realization. But death, as the line between "becoming" and "being," is radically important, because it is the moment when my free project is realized, when my free definition of myself is actualized.[30]

Whether my state of "being" is a freely-closed frustration of my identity and my powers to be open to all knowledge and love, and whether the horizon of my ultimate meaning has been freely defined as my body, my possessions, my own encapsulation, or whether I am a freely created project of openness to all that is other, all that is true and good, all that is—this will have depended upon the formation of my own life in the continuum of events and habits which I have freely assumed. This is the basis of the horror and the glory of freedom, the basis of man's great potential, the root of moral absurdity and moral dignity—ultimate openness or ultimate enclosure.

Death, in this context, then, is not properly conceived as "the end"—unless we add, "the end of the beginning, the end of the process, the end of the project-formation." Death is rather a passage to being, to completion, and to realization. It is a finishing of my "births."[31]

> The bodily energy decreases to the point where it can no longer supply adequate power to psychic and spiritual life. The body, which formerly has been a necessary condition of subjective activity, in the end becomes a hindrance. Similar situations are often found at earlier stages as well. The womb which was an absolute condition for life during the pre-natal period, becomes an obstacle (and is, no doubt, obscurely felt as such) the moment that the human being is about to be born. The same thing happens to the later, ever widening substitutes for the womb, like the mother's lap, home, family, school, group, or country. We have seen that the human being is born, grows, and attains higher stages precisely by tearing away from previous environments which have become like so many prisons.
>
> If we consider life as a series of births, the analogies of various situations force us to accept the following hypothesis, which helps to locate the asymptote of the vital curve. *Is it not true that death is another birth?* Is not this body, whose power is constantly diminishing, and indispensable but only provisional womb? Does it not have to be relinquished if the person, developed through its means, is to be born? . . .
>
> The fetus is subjected to the most painful crisis of its prenatal life precisely when it is about to be born: it is

pressed, contracted, almost strangled, and finally expelled, with no knowledge that beyond the passage there awaits it free air, space, sight, and love. Immediately before death, another great passage, man suffers the biological agony: his hold loosens; with no experience of what he is about to become, he fights for air and feels as if he were being expelled from his body. It is clear, therefore, that the positive meaning of this event cannot be revealed by the preparatory phases, the expulsion: the pains of birth are not yet birth itself, and old age and agony are not yet the stage at which the spiritual person is delivered from the material womb.[32]

Death, most certainly, is that moment at which I cease my becoming; and by the evidence at hand, most probably (if there is any fundamental meaning to human life and action) that moment at which I begin to be. Thus, the most proper way to die is the most proper way to philosophize—with one's hands open to the horizon of all that one might become, open to all of one's unconditional possibilities, open to the fullest actualization of one's identity and the absolute response to one's questioning.

Thus man's destiny is not ultimately a pursuit, but an unfolding. His goal is not a fragment on the horizon, but a God on whose fullness he draws. His basic choice is not what good to acquire, but what orientation to assume. Will he be attentive to the presence of Being? Will he respond to the invitation of the Infinite? Only by answering the gift of Self with the gift of himself can he ever fully and consciously *be* what he is. Only by animating the torrential multiplicity of his desires with the fire of a single love—a love whose term is ultimately more himself than he is himself—can he fully realize in his own life that interiority and adhesion to Being in which he participates, and that communion with Being to which he is called. Only by digging deep into value of the self will he break through to paradise.[33]

This perhaps is the final posture of the philosopher—hands open to response. Initiated in the necessity to question himself, and having discovered himself as an insatiable drive to know and love, as a pressure towards fuller and fuller being, he now again in questioning calls out for a response to his finitude, his contingency, and his questioning. His openness invites an inexhaustible source to fill him up, to give meaning to his personhood. And perhaps he is led to look somewhere for the absolute response.

A Note on Revelation

The incarnation, it seems to me, is God's response to questioning man. The "unredeemed man" is the one who in his finiteness and contingency tries to answer his own questioning by appropriation instead of love, by seeking cognitive power instead of cognitive self-transcendence, who is subject to fear and external domination instead of having true self-possession.

The "redeemed man," because of God's response as God-man, is able to find his truest and fullest identity, to achieve authentic self-actualization. In the God-man, we see that true knowledge is not power-directed but is rather openness to the Father, that love is not appropriation, but rather self-divestment, that God—as the ultimate and absolute value for man—is not tyranny, but personhood and love.

The God-man reveals that personhood is the very foundation of reality, which in the creativity of knowledge and love overflows from divine creative action into the act of man who might freely share in such a life of personhood, knowledge, and love. The absolute personhood of God, and his life of unconditional love and knowledge, is that *in which* we participate by free gift and *to which* we find ourselves "pressurized" and which is accomplished only through our own free self-gift which is our creative life-project.

The absolute paradigm and fulfillment of human openness is the person of Jesus Christ, "the unique case of the perfect fulfillment of human reality (a nature, which by giving itself fully to the mystery of fullness, so empties itself that it becomes God) which means that man only *is*, when he gives himself away."[34] Rahner is then led on to say, "Whoever accepts his human existence and his humanity (and that is most difficult) in patience, or better, in faith, hope, and love (no matter what he might call them) as the mystery that resides in the mystery of eternal love . . . is in effect saying 'yes' to Jesus Christ whether he knows it explicitly or not."[35]

THE SCANDAL OF TRUTH
Jean Daniélou[36]

It is certainly true that God's existence throws any claim of mine out of court. Yet for all that, it does not destroy my existence, but only stops my appropriation of my existence. It enjoins me to acknowledge it as received, from instant to instant. There exactly is the condition of created being. It implies a radical dependence. I do not exist save as I am (like a word) being uttered by another. And ratifying my existence means recognizing this dependence. But this comes in conflict with my passion to belong to myself. The clearsighted man grasps this very well. He knows that what is, always is *by gift*. That is why he takes refuge in non-acceptance. "This at least is mine, all mine," said Rivière of his sins.

But this declaration of my dependence should be for me the most exalting of discoveries. It means in effect that I do not exist save as I am loved. It radically destroys my solitude. To exist means my already being in connection with another. And ratifying my existence means recognizing this relationship; and responding to this gift by giving thanks means having found my way to communication. Nor is any inferiority implied by this relationship, which corresponds, instead, to the very structure of being. The Christian dogma of the Trinity expresses, in effect, this paradoxical reality; that *three* is as primordial as *one*, which is to say that love is co-eternal with existence and plays its part in the structure of being at the utter bottom of things. And hence this relative character of mine is nothing but the created epiphany of the uncreated mystery.

THEISM AND MATERIALISM
William James[37]

Theism and materialism, so indifferent when taken retro-spectively, point, when we take them prospectively, to wholly different outlooks of experience. For, according to the theory of mechanical evolution, the laws of redistribution of matter and motion, though they are certainly to thank for all the good hours which our organisms have ever yielded us and for all the ideals which our minds now frame, are yet fatally certain to undo their work again, and to redissolve everything that they have once evolved. You all know the picture of the last state of the universe, which evolutionary science foresees. I can not state it better than in Mr. Balfour's words: "The energies of our system will decay, the glory of the sun will be dimmed and the earth, tideless and inert, will no longer tolerate the race which has for a moment disturbed its solitude. Man will go down into the pit, and all his thoughts will perish. The uneasy consciousness which in this obscure corner has for a brief space broken the contented silence of the universe, will be at rest. Matter will know itself no longer. 'Imperishable monuments' and 'immortal deeds,' death itself, and love stronger than death, will be as if they had not been. Nor will anything that is, be better or worse for all that the labor, genius, devotion, and suffering of man have striven through countless ages to effect."

That is the sting of it, that in the vast driftings of the cosmic weather, though many a jewelled shore appears, and many an enchanted cloud-bank floats away, long lingering ere it be dissolved—even as our world now lingers, for our joy—yet when these transient products are gone, nothing, absolutely *nothing* remains, to represent those particular qualities, those elements of preciousness which they may have enshrined. Dead and gone are they, gone utterly from the very sphere and room of being. Without an echo; without a memory; without an influence on aught that may come after, to make it care for similar ideals. This utter final wreck and tragedy is of the essence of scientific materialism as at present understood. The lower and not the higher forces are the eternal forces, or the last surviving forces within the only cycle of evolution which we can definitely see. Mr. Spencer believes this as much as any one; so why should he argue with us as if we were making silly aesthetic objections to the "grossness" of "matter and motion," the principles of his philosophy, when what really dismays us is the disconsolateness of its ulterior practical results?

No, the true objection to materialism is not positive but negative. It would be farcical at this day to make complaint of it for what it *is*, for "grossness." Grossness is what grossness *does*—we now know *that*. We make complaint of it, on the contrary, for what it is *not*—not a permanent warrant for our more ideal interests, not a fulfiller of our remotest hopes.

The notion of God, on the other hand, however inferior it may be in clearness to those mathematical notions so current in mechanical philosophy, has at least this practical superiority over them, that it guarantees an ideal order that shall be permanently preserved. A world with a God in it to say the last word, may indeed burn up or freeze, but we then think of him as still mindful of the old ideals and sure to bring them elsewhere to fruition; so that, where he is, tragedy is only provisional and partial, and shipwreck and dissolution not the absolutely final things. This need of an eternal moral order is one of the deepest needs of our breast. And those poets, like Dante and Wordsworth, who live on the conviction of such an order, owe to that fact the extraordinary tonic and emotional and practical appeals, in these adjustments of our concrete attitudes of hope and expectation, and all the delicate consequences which their differences entail, lie the real meanings of materialism and spiritualism—not in hair-splitting abstractions about matter's inner essence, or about the metaphysical attributes of God. Materialism means simply the denial that the moral order is eternal, and the cutting off of ultimate hopes; spiritualism means the affirmation of an eternal moral order and the letting loose of hope. Surely here is an issue genuine enough, for anyone who feels it; and, as long as men are men, it will yield matter for a serious philosophic debate.

But possibly some of you may still rally to their defence. Even whilst admitting that spiritualism and materialism make different prophecies of the world's future, you may yourselves pooh-pooh the difference as something so infinitely remote as to mean nothing for a sane mind. The essence of a sane mind, you may say, is to take shorter views, and to feel no concern about such chimeras as the latter end of the world. Well, I can only say that if you say this, you do injustice to human nature. Religious melancholy is not disposed of by a simple flourish of the word insanity. The absolute things, the last things, the overlapping things, are the truly philosophic concerns; all superior minds feel seriously about them, and the mind with the shortest views is simply the mind of the more shallow man.

The issues of fact at stake in the debate are of course vaguely enough conceived by us at present. But spiritualistic faith in all its forms deals with a world of *promise,* while materialism's sun sets in a sea of disappointment. Remember what I said of the Absolute: it grants us moral holidays. Any religious view does this. It not only incites our more strenuous moments, but it also takes our joyous, careless, trustful moments, and it justifies them. It paints the grounds of justification vaguely enough, to be sure. The exact features of the saving future facts that our belief in God insures, will have to be ciphered out by the interminable methods of science: we can *study* our God only by studying his Creation. But we can *enjoy* our God, if we have one, in advance of all that labor. I myself believe that the evidence for God lies primarily in inner personal experiences. When they have once given you your God, his name means at least the benefit of the holiday. You remember what I said yesterday about the way in which truths clash and try to "down" each other. The truth of "God" has to run the gauntlet of all our other truths. It is on trial by them and they on trial by it. Our *final* opinion about God can be settled only after all the truths have straightened themselves out together. Let us hope that they shall find a *modus vivendi.*

1. Jean-Paul Sartre, *The Age of Reason*, tr. by Eve Sutton (New York: Bantam, 1959), p. 342.

2. Nicolai Berdyaev, *The Destiny of Man* from *Christian Existentialism,* tr. by Donald Lowrie (New York: Harper Torchbooks, 1965), p. 81.

3. Gabriel Marcel, *Creative Fidelity,* tr. by Robert Rosthal (New York: Noonday, 1964), p. 244.

4. James E. Royce, *Man and His Nature* (New York: McGraw-Hill 1961), p. 284.

5. If we look at a change from a living human body to a corpse, which is most probably a conglomeration of chemicals or living things, we see that what precisely specified this thing as a living human being is there no more. This has been called a substantial change because *what* the thing had been, is now a different *what*. The corpse has no more the substantial form by which it was human. Nevertheless there remains some common "stuff"—and a principle of continuity which was common to the man before death and the corpse—a principle by which the man was before death, potentially a corpse. This principle has been called prime matter. Matter is always some *kind* of matter, and that which makes it a human kind of matter, the substantial form, or human soul, is not there any more.

6. Rainer Maria Rilke, *Duinic Elegies.*

7. Blaise Pascal, *Pensées: Thoughts on Religion and Other Subjects* (New York: Washington Square Press, 1965), pp. 53-54.

8. Roger Troisfontaines, *I Do Not Die,* tr. by F. E. Albert (New York: Desclée 1963), pp. 100-101. The entire book is quite excellent and readable.

9. Jean-Paul Sartre, *Being and Nothingness,* tr. by Hazel Barnes (New York: Philosophical Library, 1956), p. 615. Note well: unfortunately the Citadel edition in paperback (cited previously) does not have this and other important passages. The editing work by M. Barnes is commendable in the Citadel edition, but many key ideas are seemingly misinterpreted (or interpreted only one way).

10. *Ibid.,* p. 627.

11. Karl Rahner, *Spiritual Exercises* (New York: Herder & Herder, 1965), p. 101.

12. *Op. cit.,* p. 244.

13. Kurt Goldstein, "Organismic Psychology" from *Psychology of Personality: Readings in Theory,* ed. W. S. Sahakian (Chicago: Rand McNally, 1965), p. 303. From Goldstein's *Human Nature in the Light of Psychopathology* (Cambridge, Mass.: Harvard University Press, 1940) pp. 5-25.

14. Andras Angyal, "Basic Principles of a Holistic Theory of Personality," in Sahakian, *op. cit.* From Angyal's *Foundations for a Science of Personality* (Cambridge, Mass: Harvard University Press, 1941) pp. 50-55.

15. Carl Rogers, "A Phenomenological Theory of Personality," in *Ibid.,* p. 475. From *Client-Centered Therapy* (Boston: Houghton Mifflin, 1951), pp. 483-524.

16. Sigmund Freud. From the *New York Times Magazine,* May 6, 1956.

17. "The Humanist Manifesto," from *The New Humanist,* May-June 1933, pp. 58-61.

18. W. T. Stace, "Man Against Darkness," *The Atlantic,* Sept. 1948.

19. Sartre, *Being and Nothingness* p. 615.

20. *Ibid.,* pp. 626, 627.

21. Albert Camus, *The Rebel,* tr. A. Bower (New York: Vintage, 1956), p. 100.

22. *Ibid.,* p. 101.

23. John J. McMahon, "Catholic Students Look at Death" from *Commonweal,* Jan. 26, 1968, p. 491

24. See Nietzche's *Beyond Good and Evil* for an indictment.

25. Fromm, *Art of Loving* and *Man for Himself.*

26. "Any activity pursued in behalf of an ideal end against obstacles and in spite of threats of personal loss because of conviction of its general and enduring value is religious in quality." See all of *A Common Faith* (New Haven: Yale University Press, 1964), p. 27.

27. Rollo May, "Existential Bases of Psychotherapy," from Maurice Friedman (ed.), *Worlds of Existentialism* (New York: Random House, 1964), p. 440. This entire book is worthwhile having, although it is still only in an expensive hard-bound edition. Short and brilliant readings.

28. Gordon Allport, *Becoming* (New Haven: Yale University Press, 1955), p. 98. The entire book is worth reading.

29. Abraham Maslow, *Toward a Psychology of Being* (Princeton, N.J.: Van Nostrand, 1962), pp. 147, 151.

30. The term "being" is used here in the sense of completion, fulfillment, or actualization rather than with any connotation of "pure act", Nor do realization and completion necessarily carry the connotation of staticity. If a man has defined himself by fidelity to the drives of understanding and love, both of which are "opended " dynamisms, his realization would seem to lie precisely in the exercise of these potentialities before and within the inexhaustible horizon of absolute knowledge and love.

31. It does not follow that every man who dies is "completed and actualized." Since man is free, he can freely choose to violate his identity. In this connection, there are interesting implications for the possible meanings of "heaven," "hell."

32. Troisfontaines, *op. cit.*, pp. 134-136.

33. Robert Johann, *The Meaning of Love* (Glen Rock, N. J.: Deus Books, 1966), pp. 79-80.

34. Karl Rahner, *The Spiritual Exercises* (New York: Herder and Herder, 1966), p. 103.

35. *Ibid.*, pp. 103-104.

36. Jean Danielou, *The Scandal of Truth,* tr. W. J. Kerrigan (Baltimore: Helicon, 1962), pp. 67-68.

37. William James, *Pragmatism and other Essays* (New York: Washington Square Press, 1963), pp. 47-50.

Adler, Mortimer J. *The Conditions of Philosophy.* New York: Delta, 1965. Treats the types of methods which should be used in philosophy. Very good on the nature of knowledge, certitude.

Allport, Gordon. *Becoming.* New Haven: Yale, 1955. A short book requiring a bit of philosophy and psychology for background.

Barrett, William. *Irrational Man.* Garden City, N. Y.: Doubleday Anchor, 1962. A good treatment (rather easy) of the existential approach to truth and the philosophy of man.

Bertocci, Peter, and Millard, Richard. *Personality and the Good.* New York: McKay, 1963. A treatment of various psychological theories and their immediate philosophical and ethical implications. Quite worthwhile, although it is only in a hardbound edition at present.

Dewey, John. *A Common Faith.* New Haven: Yale, 1964 (original 1934). A treatment of the religious attitude (as opposed to religion) and its importance for human development. See also *The Quest for Certainty,* which offers some strong objections to supernatural dualisms.

Goldbrunner, Josef. *Cure of Mind and Cure of Soul.* Notre Dame, Ind: University of Notre Dame Press, 1963. A depth-psychology treatment of the meaning of "person." The first eighty pages have many important philosophical insights.

Golding, William. *Lord of the Flies.* New York: Capricorn, 1959. A

novel which presents a fundamentally Hobbesian interpretation of man. Disturbing and well written.

James, William. *Pragmatism and Other Essays*. New York: Washington Square Press, 1963. An excellent selection of essays
dealing with the pragmatic view of man and truth. Quite
important.

Montagu, Ashley. *On Being Human*. New New York: Hawthorn
Books, 1966. From a social-anthropoligist,who has also
written many other books dealing with man—among them,
Man in Process.

Nietzsche, Friedrich. *Beyond Good and Evil*. Chicago: Gateway,
1965. A brilliant book, seemingly about morals, but more
radically about man and the nature of life as essentially
appropriative.

Nogar, Raymond. *The Wisdom of Evolution*. New York:
Mentor-Omega, 1966. A synthetic treatment of evolution and
its philosophical implications. Quite good.

Rand, Ayn. *For the New Intellectual*. New York: Signet, 1961.
Different approach to the meaning of man than we have been
emphasizing. It must be confronted and thought through.

Rogers, Carl. *On Becoming a Person*. Boston: Houghton Mifflin
Company, 1961. General synthetic presentation of Rogers's
theory.

Tournier, Paul. *The Meaning of Persons*. New York: Harper and
Row, 1957. Quite subjectively written, but valuable in insights
by a doctor-psychiatrist from Europe.

Troisfontaines, *I Do Not Die*. New York: Desclée, 1963. Excellent
book, treating the problem of immortality from a
Christian-personalist point of view.

INDEX OF TOPICS AND AUTHORS

Allport, Gordon, 139
Appetite and cognition, 44-46
Aquinas, Thomas (Thomism), 40, 42, 51-52, 61, 124-125

Buber, Martin, 8, 38-39, 'I And Thou' 38-39
de Beauvoir, Simone, 127

Camus, Albert, 84f, 134, 136
Cognition, see Knowledge

Daniélou, Jean, "Scandal of Truth," 145
Death, 131-142
Determinism, 72-76
Dewey, John, 138
Dostoevsky, Fyodor, 9, 18, 86
De Vinck, José, 110-111

Egoism—Altruism, 100-103

Frankl, Viktor, 9, 18, 84-85, 100, 103, 106-107
Freedom, 5-7, 65-99, phenomenological description 67-70; and structure, 81-83; metaphysical argument, 70-72; and anxiety, 83-87
Fromm, Erich, 102, 106, 110

Hesse, Hermann, 1, 19
Historicity and structure, 72, 81, 83
Humanism and the problem of death, 134-137
Husserl, Edmund, 22
Huxley, Aldous, 86, 97

Immortality, 127-142
Intelligence, 28-35
Intentionality, 23, 24, 34, 101
Internal sensation, 26, 28

James, William, "Theism and Materialism," 145-148
Jaspers, Karl, "What is Philosophy?" 11-16

Kierkegaard, Søren, 8, 44
Knowledge, 22-35; insatiability of, 30, 33, 34, 129, 131; sensory, 24-28; intellectual, 28, 30, 129; as other-directed, 34, 35; prior to appetite, 45-46

Language, 28, 29
Life-project, 15, 138, 141
Love, 48-50, 100-118

Marcel, Gabriel, 7, 97, 124, 131
Maslow, Abraham, 19, 40, 48ff, 66, 108, 119, 139; "Toward a Psychology of Being," 56-60
May, Rollo, 9, 20, 97, 107, 108, 139

Nature and powers, 51-53

Pascal, Blaise, 127
Personhood, 7, 10, 111-114
Philosophy as a discipline, 1-10, "What Is Philosophy?" 11-16

Playboy philosophy, 105, 107, 119
Powers and potentialities, 51-52, 123ff, 143f

Questioning, 3, 5, 67ff, 75f

Rahner, Karl, 131, 143, 144
Revelation, 143-144
Revolt and liberation, 5, 7
Rilke, Rainer Marie, 20, 126
Rogers, Carl, 54, 82, 94, 98, 131

Sartre, Jean-Paul, 65, 77-80, 81, 94, 100, 123, 130, 134, 136
Self - reflection, 31f, 67ff, 128ff
Sense knowledge, 24-28; and sense appetite, 46ff
Sexuality and human love, 103-115

Skinner, B. F., 65, 66ff, 75, 76, 79, 81, 93
Soul, 53ff, 122-145
Stace, W. T., 133

Teilhard de Chardin, Pierre, 36, 112; "Hymn of the Universe," 36-37
Transcendence, 138-143
Troisfontaines, Roger, 141ff, 154

Unity of Man, 32, 35, 51ff, 54-55, 127ff, 132
Universals, 29

Values, 46, 50, 113

Wild, John, "Freedom of Consciousness," 87-92
Wilhelmsen, F. D., "Metaphysics of Love," 115-118
Will, 51, 70, 72, 129